Men-at-Arms • 243

# Rome's Enemies (5)

## The Desert Frontier

David Nicolle • Illustrated by Angus McBride
*Series editor* Martin Windrow

First published in Great Britain in 1991 by Osprey Publishing,
Midland House, West Way, Botley, Oxford OX2 0PH, UK
44-02 23rd St, Suite 219, Long Island City, NY 11101, USA
Email: info@ospreypublishing.com

Osprey Publishing is part of the Osprey Group.

Transferred to digital print on demand 2011

First published 1991
13th impression 2008

Printed and bound by PrintOnDemand-Worldwide.com, Peterborough, UK

A CIP catalogue record for this book is available from the British Library

ISBN: 978 1 85532 166 3

Series Editor: Martin Windrow
Filmset in Great Britain

**Dedication**
For Valentina and Ashraff 'from Irbid to the Ormes'.

**Artist's note**
Readers may care to note that the original paintings from which the colour plates in this book were prepared are available for
private sale. All reproduction copyright whatsoever is retained by the Publisher. Enquiries should be addressed to:

Scorpio Gallery
PO Box 475
Hailsham
East Sussex
BN27 2SL
UK

The Publishers regret that they can enter into no correspondence upon this matter.

**The Woodland Trust**
Osprey Publishing is supporting the Woodland Trust, the UK's leading woodland conservation charity, by funding the
dedication of trees.

**www.ospreypublishing.com**

# THE DESERT FRONTIER

Rome's desert frontier was one where the Empire faced few dangers, for here relations were generally based on a mutual interest in trade across the frontier. The Berbers of North Africa were too few to be more than an occasional nuisance, while the 'threat' posed by desert nomads to the Fertile Crescent has always been exaggerated. Only when led by settled town-based people did the bedouin become a menace, rather than merely taking advantage of occasional breakdowns in authority to raid their neighbours. Nevertheless, an ending of Roman subsidies (or bribes to remain friendly) could lead to local diffi-culties. Even the doomed challenge posed by Palmyra under the formidable Queen Zenobia centred upon a wealthy desert city, a fertile oasis and vast trading links. Yet when Rome did clash with desert peoples,

particularly those of Syria and Arabia, the mobility, fighting skills and ability to withdraw into an arid wilderness often gave the Arabs, Berbers and Sudan-ese a temporary edge. Such clashes also served to change the attitudes of a declining Roman Empire from the late 3rd century AD.

The Arab–Islamic invasions of the 7th century caught Byzantium by surprise, not merely because the Byzantines had just won a costly war against their age-old Iranian enemies, but because a thousand years of history had taught them not to expect a serious threat from Arabia. The primary function of desert frontier defences had been to protect lucrative trade routes largely operated by local Semitic Arab peoples. Nor was the Roman *limes* or fortified frontier much of a barrier, since the whole idea of fixed desert defences has been doubtful throughout military history. Recent study has even indicated that many fortifications, once assumed to be Roman because of their regular planning, are actually Iranian or pre-

*Terracotta statuette of a falling Numidian warrior from southern Italy, 3–2 cents. BC. (Louvre Mus., inv. 5223, Paris)*

Berber cavalry carved in Trajan's Column in Rome, AD 113. Like so many representations of non-Roman warriors on the Column, these Berbers are probably based on hearsay and may therefore be very inaccurate.

that the militarily backward Nubians and Sudanese made was in their use of elephants.

Mediterranean influence upon the desert peoples is more obvious. Even the Arab word for sword — *sayf* — might stem from the Greek *xyphos*, while the Arabs continued to use short stabbing swords developed from the Roman infantry *gladius* well into the Middle Ages. The spear had been long a symbol of authority in Rome and was later seen among Muslim Arabs, continuing as such among the Muslim Bornu of western Sudan into modern times. Paradoxically, there was also an enormous effort by the late Roman or Byzantine Empire to convert the desert peoples to Christianity. Not only was this a religious duty but such conversions were also intended to cement an alliance. Meanwhile the rival Sassanian Empire of Iran had no new faith to offer its allies, though the Iranians did protect Jews or heretical anti-Byzantine Christians.

# CHRONOLOGY

**BC**

**146** Rome conquers and annexes Carthage (northern Tunisia.

**106** Rome annexes southern Tunisia and western Libya.

**74** Rome conquers Cyrenaica in eastern Libya

**64** Collapse of Seleucid Empire in the Middle East; Rome annexes Syria.

**63** Collapse of Maccabean Jewish dynasty; Rome occupies Palestine.

**53** Parthian Persians defeat Romans at battle of Carrhae, halt eastward expansion of Roman Empire.

**46** Rome annexes Numidia in eastern Algeria.

**40–37** Rome recognizes Herod as ruler of Judea; Herod wins control of Palestine.

**30** Rome annexes Egypt.

**23** Meroitic Sudanese invade Egypt; Rome occupies northern Nubia.

**AD**

**c. 6** Birth of Jesus Christ.

**17** Palmyra incorporated as autonomous province in Roman Syria.

**40** Rome annexes Mauretania in north-west Africa.

Islamic Arab. It has also been suggested that a zone of small forts in the south of Roman Syria had more to do with internal security than a threat from beyond the frontier. Nevertheless the military prowess of desert peoples impressed the Romans, who recruited large numbers as auxiliary cavalry and archers.

In addition to providing the Roman Army with its best archers, the Easterners (largely Arab but generally known as 'Syrians') served as Rome's most effective *dromedarii* or camel-mounted troops. The Romans, recognizing a good cavalry mount when they saw one, may also have brought the Arabian horse to Europe; while one of the few contributions

44 Rome annexes Palestine.

c. 50 Expansion of kingdom of Axum in Ethiopia.

66–73 First Jewish Revolt against Rome defeated; Temple of Jerusalem destroyed in AD 70.

105–106 Rome annexes Nabatean Petra.

129 Palmyra becomes free city within Roman Empire.

132 Second Jewish Revolt against Rome leads to Jewish 'diaspora'.

164–363 Rome conquers and occupies northern Mesopotamia (north-eastern Syria and north-western Iraq).

206 Sabaean king of south Arabia becomes ruler of almost entire Arabian peninsula; invades Iraq, defeats Parthian army.

226 Sassanians defeat Parthians; establishment of Sassanian Empire in Iraq, Iran, etc.

260 Sassanians capture Roman Emperor; also occupy southern coast of Arabian Gulf and Oman; Palmyra defeats Sassanians.

268–270 Palmyra conquers Roman Syria, Palestine and Egypt.

272–273 Romans defeat and destroy Palmyra.

285 Division of Roman Empire into eastern and western halves.

291 Decline of Sudanese kingdom of Meroe.

296 Noba/Nobatae invited by Romans to defend southern frontier of Egypt.

313 Christianity tolerated within Roman Empire.

c. 320–340 Final collapse of Meroe.

c. 340 Conversion of Axumite Ethiopia to Christianity.

c. 400 Establishment of autonomous Lakhmid Arab state on desert frontier of Sassanian Persian Empire.

429 Germanic Vandal and Iranian Alan tribes conquer Roman North Africa from Morocco to Tunisia.

c. 440 Quraysh family (ancestors of Prophet Muhammad) win control of Mecca.

502 Treaty of peace between Byzantines and Arab Kinda tribe; Arab Ghassanid tribe replaces Salih tribe as Byzantine *foederati*.

522 Ethiopians conquer Himyarite Yemen.

c. 530 Lakhmid ruler appointed 'king' of Arabian peninsula by Sassanians.

533–534 Byzantines defeat Vandals and reconquer North Africa.

541–544 Bubonic plague spreads from Egypt throughout Middle East to Europe; first recorded 'pandemic' plague in history, regularly recurs until AD 608.

543–580 Byzantine missions convert Nubia and central Sudan to Christianity.

c. 570 Ethiopian governor of Yemen and Arab Kinda allies in campaign to extend Ethiopian authority in Arabia; birth of Prophet Muhammad.

c. 574 Sassanian Persians conquer Yemen; direct rule imposed in 597.

(c. 600 Establishment of Ghana, first known state in West Africa.)

602 Sassanian abolition of autonomous Lakhmid Arab frontier state in Iraq.

612–628 Sassanian Persian conquest of Syria, Egypt and part of Anatolia.

627 Byzantines defeat Sassanians.

629–630 First Muslim incursion into southern Jordan.

632 Death of Prophet Muhammad.

632–633 Muslims lose and regain control of Arabian Peninsula.

*Meroitic relief carving of archers carrying ankhs, the ancient Egyptian symbols of life. Their bows are far smaller than in reality, 1–3 cents. AD. (Brooklyn Mus., no. 76.8, New York)*

**634–642** Muslim conquest of Syria, Egypt and Iraq, later also Iran, etc.

**642–705** Muslim conquest of North Africa, later also Spain.

# NORTH AFRICA

After the fall of Carthage to Rome, the rest of unoccupied North Africa consisted of Berber tribal states. These fought against Roman annexation but were too weak to put up an effective resistance. Although there were numerous revolts, most tribes within the Empire were demilitarized, while some furnished the Roman Army with local militias and auxiliary troops.

In the 3rd century AD the Emperor Diocletian undertook extensive military reforms throughout the Empire, after which warlike frontier peoples like the Berbers played a more important role as semi-autonomous *foederati* under their own military leaders. But the story of such troops really forms part of the late Roman Army (see forthcoming MAA, *Romano-Byzantine Armies 4th–9th Century*. On the other hand, increasing resistance by the Berbers had greatly weakened Rome's hold by the time the Germanic Vandals erupted on the scene in the 5th century. Thereafter the Berbers reverted to their warrior traditions, growing in power at the expense of the Vandal newcomers. Berber forces also played a major role in the Romano-Byzantine reconquest, and Berber tribes dominated the entire area except for some Byzantine-ruled coastal regions by the time of the Arab–Islamic invasion.

The situation in the eastern province of North Africa (now eastern Libya) was slightly different. Here the population was already partly Arabized and certainly had numerous camels—unlike the rest of North Africa—by the 7th century. An even more striking situation may have existed far to the west in northern Morocco. Here the Jewish Birghwata Berbers seem to have established a little-known state which may have been raiding Visigothic Spain in collaboration with co-religionists in the Iberian Peninsula long before the Muslim Arab and Berber conquest of that country in AD 711.

Though Berber resistance was ineffective, Berber armies were more than mere tribal bands and later Berber organization was inevitably more advanced. The basic social unit seems to have been the *ikh* or 'people', consisting of several families. Two or three *ikhs* inhabited a village, a dozen or so villages forming a tribe which defended its own territory. In the face of external threats, tribes could form a *leff* or *sof* confederation under a temporary elected military chief. Small tribes were normally led by elders, but larger tribal units were ruled by kings, some of whom founded local dynasties (which were, however, overthrown by the Romans). Others reappeared

*Relief carving of Prince Arikankharer, from Meroe, c. AD 25–41 (Art Mus., inv. 1922.145, Worcester, USA)*

*Bronze statuette of a bound prisoner: Meroitic, 1 cent. AD. This unfortunate individual probably represents one of Meroe's tribal foes to the south, east or west. (British Mus., inv. 65222, London)*

later, while obscure Berber 'nations' gave the invading Muslim Arabs a hard fight in the 7th century.

In the mountains these Berbers led a settled agricultural way of life, many villages even being defended by simple towers. Here most warriors fought on foot; but in the steppes the tribes were nomadic, raising large numbers of horses and fighting as cavalry. Less is known about the peoples of the Sahara Desert. In the 10th century they were described as similar to the inhabitants of southern Morocco though also having close links with what is now the western Sudan. Militarily the most important tribes were clearly the steppe nomads. The nomadic way of life also increased from the 4th century onwards, probably as a result of camels having been introduced by Syrian troops in Roman service a few centuries earlier. Nevertheless the only nomads to rely primarily on camels, even at the end of the Byzantine period, were those of what is now Libya.

Despite changes over the centuries there was remarkable continuity in Berber weapons and tactics. In pre-Roman Numidia tribal troops followed their own leaders, with those closest to the ruler forming the bulk of his army. Such forces could be raised quickly, but also melted away at sowing or harvesting

*These archers carved on the Arch of Constantine in Rome probably represent the Blemmye warriors from Nubia who fought in Constantine's army. Note how the perhaps poisoned arrows are thrust through their head-bands.*

time. The best tribal troops were horsemen, each aristocratic warrior being followed by his servants. Yet the most powerful kings of Numidia also raised an élite force of slaves, freedmen and mercenaries paid through taxation. Such formations were based upon the Roman or Carthaginian model and even included infantry 'legions'. Little is known of their origins, though they included Thracians and Italians.

At first these North African armies faced the

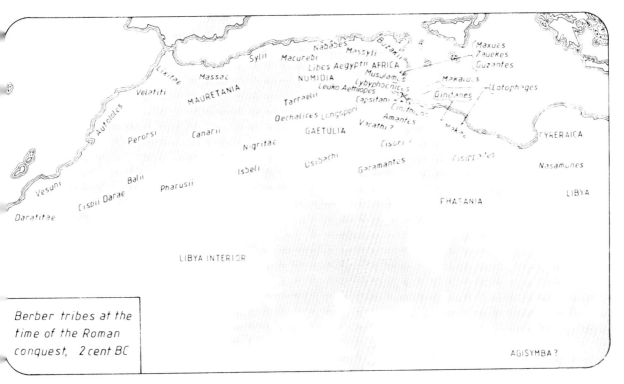

Berber tribes at the time of the Roman conquest, 2 cent BC

▲ Though very damaged, the sword carried by the Archangel Gabriel in this Nubian wall painting of c. AD 710 is distinctive. It lacks any form of cross-guard, and has features in common with weapons of the preceding 'X-Group' culture of Nubia, and with those shown on pre-Islamic Yemeni carvings. As such the sword may represent a weapon common to peoples on both sides of the southern Red Sea from the 5th to 8th centuries. The painting comes from the ruined cathedral at Faras. (National Mus., no. 234038, Warsaw)

Romans in open battle, but later resorted to raids and ambushes, often of mounted infantry operating from the mountains or of cavalry from the steppes or desert fringe. When facing Roman or Byzantine troops Berber guerrillas tried to ambush the enemy in terrain of their own choosing, preferably trapping them in a narrow place or attacking suddenly from all sides. The Berbers also knew enough to hold back some troops as a reserve or to take advantage of a success. Meanwhile their cavalry were organized into loose 'squadrons'. One problem facing the Romans was, in fact, the sheer number of horses which these Berbers could raise—up to 100,000 per year according to one report. The Romans also regarded the Berbers as brave and mobile, but unreliable, lightly armed, lacking stamina and superstitious. If themselves attacked, the Berbers retreated to mountain tops, where they built wooden field defences. I

▼ Weaponry of the African frontier: (A–E) Upper part of Numidian helmet, sword & reconstructed scabbard, spearhead & two javelins, 2–1 cents. BC, from Al Sumaa (Nat. Mus., Algiers); (F) decorated silver archer's bracer & method of holding bracer, from Ballana tombs, 'X-Group', 4 cent. AD (Archaeol. Mus., Cairo); (G) bronze quiver from Meroe, 3–5 cents. AD (Nat. Mus., Khartoum); (H–L) iron spearheads with silver-decorated sockets from Ballana tombs, 'X-Group', 4 cent. AD (Archaeol. Mus., Cairo); (M) archer's stone thumb-ring from Ballana tombs, 'X-Group', 4 cent. AD; (N) archer's stone thumb-ring from Meroe, 3–5 cents. AD (O–S) spear & arrowheads from Meroe, 3–5 cents. AD (T–U) short swords in decorated leather scabbards from Ballana tombs, 'X-Group', 4 cent. AD (Archaeol. Mus., Cairo).

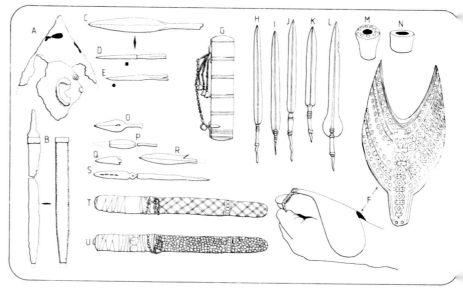

caught in open terrain they could also construct a defence for their families and flocks, where, if necessary, the women and children would also fight with slings. Meanwhile the horsemen could attack from mountain-top strongpoints, though in open terrain they often took up position some way away, striking their foes in the flank if they attacked the camp.

In later centuries, with a greater use of camels, the eastern Berber tribes would make these beasts kneel in a huge circle as a barrier against cavalry, whose horses tended to fear the camels. Other animals could also be roped together as an inner barrier, while calthrops were scattered outside. Some warriors defended the living perimeter using spears as pikes, while javelin throwers stood between the camels. The best cavalry again took up position some way away.

The Garamantes of southern Libya used four-horse chariots in ancient times, possibly as manoeuvrable archery platforms or to overawe people further south whom they raided for slaves, but such tactics are unlikely to have survived into the Roman period. The Garamantes also used horses, though to survive in the desert each animal had to carry its own water supply in skins slung beneath its belly. Not until the coming of the camel in the Middle Ages did the Sahara change from a terrifying barrier into a sand-sea navigated by great trading caravans. Prior to that the peoples of the desert fought on foot in ranks armed with pikes and javelins. It is also possible that some tribes along the southern fringe of the Sahara used war elephants, as did the people of the Nilotic Sudan and Ethiopia.

Broad-bladed javelins rather than bows were the missile weapons of all North African and west Saharan peoples. The better equipped had swords, mostly captured from the Romans. Latin sources made much of Berber 'bareback' horsemen, who rode 'without reins'. They also appear on Trajan's Column, though these carvings were probably based on hearsay rather than visual evidence. It seems more likely that Berber horsemen rode on saddle-cloths rather than the partly framed saddles of Rome, and guided their horses with a *bozal*: this is a leather or rope bridle to which a lead-rein is attached without using a metal bit in the horse's mouth. Berber shields seem to have been of leather, but whereas early Roman writers state that these were small and round,

Pre-Islamic South Arabian carved relief of warriors with spears. The man on the right also has an apparently curved sword with an angled grip. The weapon's blade has features in common with that of the Archangel Gabriel on the Nubian wall painting. (National Mus., no. 31.300.1647, Sana'a)

by the early medieval period many Berbers used very large rectangular leather shields known as *lamt*. Such shields may have originated in Ethiopia or Nilotic Sudan. In this case their spread across the length of the Sahara could be linked with the migration of the Lamtuna Berbers, ancestors of the Tuareg—the famous 'veiled men' of the Sahara.

One ancient Berber warrior custom which survived into medieval times was that of shaving part of the head before battle. Another Berber fashion was the wearing of soft goat-skin cloaks and long, flowing unbelted tunics; in Roman times these only reached the knees, but grew longer during the Muslim Middle Ages. The hooded cloak or *burnus*, which is still characteristic of North Africa, might be based upon the Roman legionary's *sagum* cloak, but the traditional *litham* or man's face veil seen until modern times owed nothing to Arab-Islamic, Roman or Carthaginian influence.

### The Nile Valley

Following the Roman occupation of Egypt the Empire's frontier reached Nubia, beyond which lay the Meroitic Kingdom of central Sudan. Between the two was the Dodekaschoenos, a region stretching from Aswan to Kosha (which has now been almost

*Carved relief of warriors fighting lions, 3 cent., from Zafar near Yarim, Yemen.* *(Present location unknown, Prof. P. Costa photograph)*

entirely flooded by the Aswan High Dam). This Rome also seized. The desert between the Nile and Red Sea was partly inhabited by Arabs in the north and Blemmye (the present-day Beja people) in the south, while deserts west of the Nile but south of a chain of oases (now known as the New Valley) were virtually uninhabited. After an initial clash between Rome and Meroe, relations remained peaceful for several centuries, but by the 3rd century Meroe was in decline. The Blemmye nomads raided Nubia and southern Egypt; in reply Rome withdrew from the Dodekaschoenos and invited a new people to defend the area. These were the Noba (present-day Nubians), who probably came from Kordofan in western Sudan, further isolating Meroe.

The kingdoms south of Roman Egypt were in some ways more highly developed than those of Berber North Africa, although iron-working had only reached Meroe in the 4th century BC. In other respects Meroe remained within the ancient Egyptian tradition, and the fall of Meroe spelled the real end of Pharaonic civilization. Christian cultures which emerged in the same parts of Sudan a few centuries later had almost nothing in common with the Meroitic past, and a kind of 'Dark Age' filled the gap. Even the names of some peoples remain unknown, although they have left magnificent archaeological relics. During this period the Noba

(Nubians) came from the west and the Blemmye (Beja) from the east to compete with a third people—'the X Group'—for control of the fertile Nile valley. It is also possible that this 'X Group' was simply an amalgamation of Noba and Blemmye.

One fact was probably crucial: the arrival of the camel—perhaps in the 2nd century AD—which gave the nomads a significant economic, political and military advantage. They became powerful long-distance raiders and traders ruled by military aristocracies. Where once Nubia and the Nile had been the only practical link across the Sahara, the nomads grew rich through trade, while Nubia slowly declined in importance. Of course the settled peoples also had camels, but only the nomads could raise them in great numbers for use in peace and war. The best camel-breeding regions were those of the Blemmye. Though primitive and largely pagan until Islamic times, the warlike Blemmye established a state in which Greek administrative terms and even some aspects of ancient Egyptian culture could be found. Blemmye archers were recruited by Romans and Byzantines, seeing service in Yemen and later against the Muslim-Arabs.

*Underground entrance into the pre-Islamic fortress of Qalaat al Kisra in Oman, looking towards the outside. The castle looms over the town of* *Rustaq, which was probably known as Suq Oman, 'Market of Oman', under Sassanian rule. (Author's photograph)*

Meanwhile the Noba (Nubians) adopted Christianity in another example of the Romano-Byzantine Empire using religion to cement an alliance. Three Nubian states now emerged: Nobadia in what had been the Dodekaschoenos, Makuria around Meroe, and Alwa, with its capital at Soba, not far from modern Khartoum. Byzantine Greek features were obvious in Nubian court ceremonial and administration, while there may also have been a small Iranian influence on Nubian archery techniques. Yet it was Egyptian Christianity which remained the dominant outside influence until the Sudan was converted to Islam in the late Middle Ages. Archaeologists have even found an early 8th-century church in distant Darfur, south of the Sahara in the far west of Sudan, while the 10th-century Arab geographer Ibn Hawqal stated that the people of what is now eastern Chad were Christian in his lifetime.

Today the only black African people to retain the Christianity brought by Byzantine missionaries from Egypt are, of course, the Ethiopians. Theirs was the southernmost Nile kingdom of the Romano-Byzantine period. Axum, as it was then known, officially converted to Christianity in the 4th century and was seen by Byzantium as an important new power in the Red Sea region. Northern influence was, however, minimal except in matters of religion, and Axum seems to have had more in common with Yemen in Arabia.

'Battle between Sassanian and Arab–Ethiopian armies' on an embroidered textile, probably 5–6 cents. AD, from Egypt or Mesopotamia. The Iranians are mounted archers, with their emperor seated at the centre holding a sword. The Ethiopian is a black African with a broad sword. The Arab on the far left is unarmoured and carries a small round shield, while others hide behind rocks near the top. (Musée des Tissus, Lyons)

### Armies of the Nile Valley states

Meroe was an agricultural but urbanized state drawing great wealth from trade. Though occasionally involved in wars Meroe was generally peaceable, while its rulers were more interested in the African south than the Roman north. Many of its warriors still used bronze weapons, some perhaps imported from Egypt, and although swords appear in Meroitic art none have yet been found. Spears and bows were the preferred weapons, while Meroe's archers used leather quivers, plus iron- and even stone-tipped arrows of wood or cane, often poisoned. Judging by other aspects of Meroitic administration the army was probably well organized, although a rare description of a late Meroitic army in action against Roman troops has them poorly marshalled behind large oxhide shields with axes, spears and the occasional sword. Many men were tattooed and also scarred

their faces, as some Sudanese still do. Elephants were used ceremonially and occasionally in war. Such animals may have been of the now-extinct North African or Saharan type, as the true African elephant is regarded as untrainable. Meroitic fortifications could be built upon earlier Egyptian structures, as at Qasr Ibrim in Nubia, or could consist of massive three-storey whitewashed mud-brick citadels as at Karanog.

The warlike Blemmye (Beja) had generally lived in a mutually beneficial, symbiotic relationship with the peoples of the fertile river banks, their nomadic society being built around family groups, each with their herd of animals. Yet when the Blemmye eventually established their own organized kingdom they used the Meroitic model. Their formidable camel-mounted armies clad in wild animal skins, armed with spears and bows, joined Queen Zenobia of Palmyra's invasion of Egypt in AD 270. Even in the 10th century Beja archers still used the poisoned arrows of their Blemmye and Meroitic predecessors. Blemmye raiders roamed the Red Sea, sometimes in captured Byzantine ships. One group hoped to attack Clysma (near modern Suez), but eventually settled for scaling the walls of a Christian monastery in Sinai using the trunks of palm trees they had chopped down.

The Blemmyes' northern border remains unclear, but it seems likely that they merged with the existing inhabitants of Nubia to create the mysterious 'X Group' culture. The military élite of this obscure people were rich, judging from the solid silver bridles and horse harness decorated with cowrie shells found in their tombs at Ballana. Here the most common weapons were very large spears, some decorated with silver, semi-precious stones and enamel. The swords were, however, small slashing weapons with blades identical to round-tipped weapons seen in early Byzantine and early Islamic art. Highly decorated archery equipment was also found, together with thumb-rings and bracers. A unique design of silver horse bit has been seen as a mystery, yet its form recalls the all-rope or leather *bozal*. Could such a bit have evolved from the *bozal* which earlier North African horsemen might have used (see above)?

With the coming of the Noba (Nubians) in the late 3rd and 4th centuries, three new kingdoms emerged in the Nile valley. But clashes between the riverine Noba and desert Blemmye continued, the victory of a certain Nubian King Silko over a King Phonen of the Blemmye being one of very few events to pass into written history. Yet Noba and Blemmye could also combine to raid Egypt, as they did in the 5th century. Shortly after the Noba (Nubians) were converted to Christianity their central Kingdom of Makuria took over the northern state of Nobatia. Here the northern defences depended upon garrisons at Kosha and Takoaa, while the region between, still known as the Batn al Hajar (Belly of Stones), provided defence in depth against Romano-Byzantine counter-raids. The governor or sub-king of this autonomous military zone, originally the Dodekaschoenos and latterly the separate state of Nobatia, was still known as the Lord of Horses. Like twelve other sub-kings, he recognized an 'over-king' at Old Dongola, a ruler who—unless he spilled human blood—was also a Christian priest. The best description of the Nubian ruler and his army comes from the 10th century, when al Mas'udi said: 'Their king rides a fine bred horse but the people are mounted on mares of small size. They fight with curiously shaped bows and it was from them that the tribes of the Hijaz and Yemen (in Arabia) and the other Arab tribes adopted the use of the bow.'

Arabs also called these Nubians 'archers of the eyes' because of their accuracy, being able to shoot a foe through the eye-slits of his helmet. Nubian bows were probably of simple wood construction like those of 20th century most ancient Egyptians, though they may also have used massive longbows like those of 20th century East African elephant poachers.

The rich southern Christian Nubian kingdom of Alwa is only now being uncovered by archaeologists. There were gold mines near the Ethiopian border, tribes as far west as Chad recognized its authority, and a flourishing slave trade fed upon more backward peoples to the south. Little is known of Alwa's army, though the kingdom's fame as a horse-breeding area must have given its warriors an advantage over their pagan victims—in fact the only piece of medieval African horse-armour yet known was recently found at Soba. During the Middle Ages the Sudan also had its own arms industry at an early date and, like the neighbouring Beja and even the central Saharan oases, exported poor-quality weapons to Egypt.

Among the most primitive peoples of the north-eastern Sudan were the mysterious 'Troglodytes', as they were known to Greeks and Romans. These cave-

*Fragment of a bronze statuette from the Kinda capital of Qaryat al Fau, 1–5 cents. AD. The art of pre-Islamic central Arabia is only now being discovered. This figure wears typical costume of the ancient Arabs, consisting of two large pieces of fabric, while his stylized hair seems similar to that shown in Yemeni art. Another bronze fragment, possibly from the same statuette, includes the fringed hem of such a costume. (University Mus., Riyadh)*

dwellers inhabited the mountainous African shore of the Red Sea and may have been related to the Blemmye people. They sometimes clashed with Roman exploratory columns. Troglodyte infantry were described by a member of one such expedition as being drawn up across the desert together with their Ethiopian allies, standing to await the onslaught of Roman cavalry. The outcome was not, however, recorded.

The Ethiopians were more interested in trade with Yemen and India than with the Nile valley. In fact the ruling class, with its capital at Axum, was itself probably of south Arabian origin. These Ethiopians regarded their monarchy as the oldest in the world. In pagan times the king was said to be descended from the God of War, but once converted to Christianity in the 4th century the Ethiopian rulers adopted King Solomon and the Queen of Sheba as their forebears. The early Byzantines, who saw Ethiopia as a valuable ally, also noted some aspects of their weaponry and organization, as did the early Muslims. Elephants, for example, were still abundant in what is now Eritrea and formed the front rank of various Ethiopian armies, the leather towers on their backs holding six men. War elephants largely disappeared from Ethiopian armies during the 6th century, but at least one accompanied a force which attempted to attack Mecca in Arabia in the year of the Prophet Muhammad's birth, c. AD 570. It caused such a sensation that the date was henceforth known as 'The Year of the Elephant'. A Byzantine ambassador who saw the Ethiopian governor of Yemen in AD 530 stated that: 'He stood above four elephants which bore a platform with four wheels and above it was a high cart bound around with gold leaves. . . . He stood there holding a small gilded shield, two little gilded spears were in his hands, and all his nobles were there, armed, while flutes made music for singing.'

An ancient Arab poem similarly described the guards of the Ethiopian governor in Yemen:

'The sons of Abyssinia around him,
Wrapped in Abyssinian silk cloth,
With white faces and black faces,
Their hair like long peppers.'

The white-faced warriors would have been the relatively light-skinned Amharic Ethiopians or their Yemeni supporters, the black-faced being African

The Nabataean capital of Petra had few man-made fortifications as the city was surrounded by near-vertical mountains. The main access road ran for about two kilometres through this narrow cleft known as the Siq. A small stream also flowed through a channel along one side of this winding passage. (Author's photograph)

slaves or tribal troops, while 'peppers' referred to hair drawn into long ringlets like that of the Beja 'Fuzzy-Wuzzies', who gave the British such a tough time in the Sudan.

By the 4th century AD the Ethiopian army was a formidable force. Its full-time regulars were known as *sarawit* 'divisions' in early Arab sources, while there were great numbers of auxiliary *ihzab* or 'supporters' from subject tribes. At first few camels were used, but they may later have become more important than the spectacular elephants. Here Ethiopian tactics were probably learned from the Blemmye (Beja) who, like the eastern Berbers, drew their camels into a circular living rampart when attacked in the open. The only horsemen in the Ethiopian army in Yemen seem to have been officers, while their infantry fought with javelins. Here in Yemen the Ethiopian army also suffered mutinies caused by dissension between its wealthy leadership

# SOUTHERN ARABIA

Relief carvings on the Temenos Gate at Petra, 2 cent. AD. Though these date from shortly after the Roman annexation of Petra, they show a warrior or deity carrying javelins in the Syrian manner rather than armed as a Roman. This is, in fact, an extremely rare example of figural art from Petra. (Author's photograph)

Semitic but non-Arab peoples, as well as Arabs, inhabited Yemen, Dhufar and Oman in the pre-Islamic period. Some preserve their separate languages to this day, although most have adopted the Arab genealogies characteristic of large parts of the modern Arabized world. Along the Omani coast were people known as *bayasirah*, said to be descended from sailors recruited in Sind (now southern Pakistan); in reality they were probably vestiges of earlier Semitic, Indo-Aryan or even Dravidian populations. Southern Arabia was in close contact with the outside world, Graeco-Roman and Iranian as well as local Arab influence being seen in social or political organization. The fame of 'Indian' swords, perhaps made locally from superior Indian *wootz* steel ingots, lingered well into the Middle Ages. Roman troops also reached central Yemen in the 1st century BC, leaving a garrison near the great pre-Islamic city of Marib—though they were soon soundly defeated.

The early history of what is now Yemen remains full of mysteries. The famous 'collapse of the Marib Dam' was credited in Arabian legend with the fall of south Arabian civilization as well as massive tribal movements throughout the Arabian Peninsula; in fact the two recorded collapses were symptoms of decline rather than its cause. The Ethiopian conquest of Yemen, and its defeat by a pro-Sassanian native revival is well documented. But the degree of subsequent Sassanian authority over southern Yemen and the way this petered out shortly before the coming of Islam is far less clear. The same is true of Sassanian Iranian rule in Oman. This dated from the 6th century, and followed a perhaps mythical domination of Oman by the pro-Sassanian Lakhmid Arabs of Iraq a century earlier.

One factor dominated the history of pre-Islamic Arabia, and that was the struggle between north and south. Until the early 5th century AD the south was dominant, virtually controlling the rich sea lanes from the Mediterranean towards India and China. But around the year AD 400 the Sassanians struck back by encouraging the northern Arab leader Imru's Qays, founder of the Lakhmid dynasty, to dominate

and the poorer rank and file. Nor could Ethiopia transport forces across the Red Sea without help from Byzantine ships, though Byzantium was of course happy to help an ally fight its proxy-war against allies of Sassanian Iran. The Ethiopian Kingdom of Axum survived for many centuries and the country remains partly Christian to this day; yet the coming of Islam would turn the Red Sea into an Arab lake, virtually isolating Ethiopia from the Mediterranean world which had given it its distinctive religion three centuries earlier.

the entire Arabian Peninsula. It was this Lakhmid-Sassanian domination of the trade routes that led Byzantium to encourage its proxy, Ethiopia, to invade Arabia, where they found regional allies including the powerful Kinda tribe of central Arabia. The Ethiopians also built a church in Sana'a, capital of Yemen, to rival the still pagan Kaaba in Mecca—a structure which would soon become the very heart of Islam. Meanwhile a massacre of Christians at Najran in AD 523–24 was a local backlash against the slaughter of Yemeni Jews and pagans by Ethiopian occupation forces. In ancient times Yemen had been ruled by priest-kings or *mukarribs*, though this system had now developed into a secular monarchy. But as central authority declined after the 1st century AD, regional *qayls* or 'dukes' became the real source of power over a local *ashraf* nobility. Each had their own tribal territory and their military help to the central government depended on the power of the king. Yemen was also known for its weapons industry, while the city of Najran was famous for armour, much of which may have been of hardened leather. Oman, the region around present-day Riyadh and the Gulf coast (then known as Yamama and Bahrain) similarly produced highly regarded military equipment. Under normal conditions the rulers of Yemen were strong enough to keep the local nomads in order and to use them as a source of good fighting men. Stronger Yemeni kings also maintained regular forces, mostly infantry plus a mobile élite of camel-mounted troops. Like the Ethiopians but unlike northern Arabs, Yemeni infantry fought with javelins, though swords were more abundant than in Africa.

The ruins of a Nabataean Temple and way-station at al Qasr, halfway between Petra and Amman. A number of such massive temples were built by the Nabataeans along their main trade routes, often in very isolated spots. (Author's photograph)

In other ways the military systems of southern Arabia were remarkably backward, horses probably not reaching the area before the 2nd century AD. In fact the most useful help that the Sassanians could send their south Arabian allies was a unit of *asawira* armoured cavalry. The traditional battle plan of the Himyarite Yemeni kings has also been preserved in a unique 13th-century Persian document (see MAA 125, *The Armies of Islam 7th–11th Centuries*, p. 5). Here a minor role is given to a very small number of horsemen. Another fascinating infantry tactic credited to a pre-Islamic Yemeni army during its attack on Yamama is astonishingly similar to one in Shakespeare's *Macbeth*: here a force crept close to the enemy's walls by camouflaging themselves with the branches of trees.

It has often been said that the ancient Arabs had no

A procession of nobles on a carved relief from Palmyra, AD 100–150. Horse and camel harnesses are elaborately decorated. While the horsemen have bow-cases and quivers attached to the rear of their saddles, the ends of the spears attached to the camel saddles can also be seen between these animals' legs. (Cleveland Museum of Art, Wade Fund 70.15, Cleveland, USA)

*The only known 'portrait' of Zenobia, the warrior Queen of Palmyra, appears on a coin minted during Palmyra's brief occupation of Egypt. (British Museum, Dept. of Coins & Medals, London)*

# CENTRAL ARABIA

knowledge of fortification or siege warfare, but this is an exaggeration for northern Arabia, and simply wrong where the south is concerned. Powerful pre-Islamic citadels still dot southern and western Arabia and invading Ethiopians had to attack many such defences. The ruins of castles traditionally built during campaigns against the Ethiopians survive along Yemen's Red Sea coast, while south of Mecca the ancient Saudi Arabian towns of Taif and Jarash were certainly walled in the 7th century. At Taif, however, the wall enclosed a large area in which different tribal groups inhabited separate hamlets, leaving plenty of open ground where their flocks could graze.

Oman differed from Yemen in various respects. A large immigration by central Arabian tribes, who then converted to Christianity in the 6th century, was followed by the installation of a Sassanian garrison of up to 4,000 troops under an Iranian *marzuban* (governor) at Sohar. A political adviser may also have been based in the great fortress of Qala'at al Kisra at Rustaq in the mountains. Like the rest of the Sassanian Empire, Oman was essentially feudal. Beneath a resident Persian military élite of *asawira* armoured cavalry, local Arab governors known as *julanda* gathered taxes from the tribes. Coastal Omanis provided the best sailors in the Sassanian fleet and already had close links with East Africa, or Zanj as it was then known. Following their fall from power many Omani *julanda* apparently migrated to Zanj in the 8th century, so reinforcing an already strong connection between Arabia and East Africa.

One modern theory suggests that the nomadic bedouin way of life only dated from the 4th century AD, and followed the collapse of desert kingdoms like Nabatean Petra or Palmyra. Other scholars argue that all the main features of bedouin society existed at least by the 5th century BC. Most, however, agree on certain aspects of life in the Arabian desert. Nomads depended upon settled peoples for metals, and thus for most weaponry, while possession of even a few horses gave the military élite an edge over tribal rivals. Sheep-raising nomads of the steppe-like desert fringe, though often wealthier than the camel-raisers of the deep desert, were vulnerable to the latter because their flocks were less mobile. In turn the sheep nomads often dominated the farming folk of the oases, whose crops or palm groves they could threaten to cut down. At the very bottom of the pecking order were itinerant 'tinker' tribes of supposedly impure descent.

Seemingly powerless 'sacred enclaves', of which pre-Islamic Mecca was the most famous, gave a religious status to tribes that controlled them, though their religious leadership still relied on the military clout of allied tribes. In addition to the pagans there were large Christian and Jewish Arab communities who were fully integrated into Arabian society. The most famous Jewish leader was, in fact, Dhu Nuwas, a 6th-century Yemeni king who persecuted Christian Arabs with gusto. Three Jewish Arab tribes of the northern Hijaz were also powerful in the early 7th century—the Qaynuqa, Quraiza and Nadhir. The first alone had 700 warriors, half of them fully mailed. Further north, near the Byzantine frontier, there were other Jewish and Christian Arab communities. Pagans, Jews and Christians took an active part in the flourishing caravan trade, many also owning property in Byzantine cities like Gaza or Damascus. Yet the merchant families, however rich, remained well armed and warlike, defending their rich caravans in the dangerous desert and competing with rivals. Neither were the tribes cut off culturally from the outside world: for example, a description of an idol of the pagan god Manat, cleared from the Kaaba by the

the Muslim faith in what many still regard as an isolated corner of the world. It is also worth noting that the first Muslims only sought to extend their religion, and thus their authority, among fellow Arabs. Unfortunately some Arab tribes lived within Byzantine or Sassanian spheres of influence, and this inevitably led the Muslims to clash with their huge imperial neighbours.

## Central Arabian Armies

Traditional Arab warfare consisted of *razzias* or raids to increase a warrior's reputation for bravery and to increase the tribe's herds. Animals could then be generously given away as gifts—which again enhanced a man's reputation. Other clashes involved access to water supplies. Such wars were generally small-scale and localized, while casualties were low and even avoided. To retreat or bow in the face of superior force was normal rather than disgraceful,

▲ *Palmyrene relief carving of the gods 'Arsu and 'Aziz, 2–3 cents. AD. They are as usual shown in Arab costume, armed with spears, swords and shields, but not wearing armour. (Archaeological Mus., inv. 7230, Palmyra)*

▼ *Here another Palmyrene warrior god, Shadrafa, has a spear, sword and shield, but also wears a lamellar cuirass of somewhat Hellenistic pattern. This carved relief was dedicated by a certain Atenatan son of Zabde'atan in AD 55. (British Mus., inv. 125206, London)*

Prophet Muhammad, stated that it wore 'a double cuirass of iron upon which were two precious swords'. This sounds remarkably like a statue of a pagan war-god from Palmyra.

The Arabs, as relatively weak players in the struggles of the ancient Middle East, tried to balance the two huge empires of Rome and Iran one against the other. Meanwhile central Arabia had been dominated by the Kinda tribal confederation since the 1st century AD. The Kinda state was largely nomadic, though it also included agricultural groups. Another trading tribe within the confederation was the Tamim, who had particularly close links with the Lakhmids of Iraq and with Mecca, where the Sassanians may still have had some political leverage in the 6th century. Nevertheless Sassanian prestige was declining while specifically Arab power centres emerged, often around *sharif* or noble families which had exercised local authority for generations. One such were the Quraysh of Mecca, a rich merchant family who were also traditional custodians of the Kaaba shrine. Such factors, as well as Divine inspiration, lay behind the astonishing emergence of

while the use of clever tactics, ruses or subterfuge was almost more admired than brute strength or physical courage. Arab warfare was, in fact, sophisticated compared to that of Rome's other frontier foes except the Iranians.

The Arabs were also eager to learn from their neighbours, and it sometimes seems as if hair styles alone distinguished them from their enemies! Arabs wore their hair very long compared to the shaven-headed Romans, and they sported trimmed beards compared to the shaven chins and long moustaches of the Persians. In reality, of course, indigenous Arab costume was also distinctive. It consisted of one or two sheet-like *izar* wraps wound around the body as mantle, loin and waist-cloths. Variations of this simple costume were worn in southern Arabia into modern times and it still forms the basis of the Muslim pilgrim's state of *ihram* or symbolic purity. Greek tunics and Persian-inspired *sirwal* trousers were also worn in areas under Byzantine or Sassanian influence. The *imama* turban had been worn since pre-Islamic times, when it was, however, a simple strip of cloth wound around the head. The *taylasan* head-shawl was more characteristic of Arabian Jews, while the tall *tartur* cap had been copied from the Arameans of the Fertile Crescent.

The invention of iron armour was attributed to the Jewish kings David and Solomon. In fact the Jewish tribes of the northern Hijaz had notably well-armed forces, surrendering 1,840 swords, 350 armours, 1,000 spears and 1,500 shields but only 50 helmets when defeated by the first Muslim armies. The Christian Arab governor of Daumat al Jandal similarly handed over 1,000 camels, 800 slaves, 400 armours and 400 spears, while the rich merchant families of Mecca also owned large arsenals. Some weaponry came from Byzantine Syria and much from Sassanian Iran, either supplied to allied tribes or captured as booty.

Black African troops, mercenaries or slaves, were recorded in the early 7th-century Hijaz, their favoured weapons being javelins, swords and shields. Javelin-armed *ahabish* mercenaries may have been of Eritrean origin, but could also have included local Arab warriors. They formed an important element in the rich Meccan army, as did freelance tribal irre-

◄ *Statue of a Palmyrene nobleman wearing Parthian-style clothes, including leggings supported by metallic suspenders. (Archaeological Mus., Palmyra)*

▶ *Relief carving of a camel rider with various pieces of equipment or weapons suspended from his saddle, 1–3 cents. AD. (Nat. Mus., Damascus)*

gulars, while Mecca raised special taxes to pay professional caravan and market guards.

The traditional Arabian *khamis* or 'five division' army structure stemmed from ancient Semitic tradition rather than reflecting Greek influence. Each tribal unit had its own flags called *raya* or *liwa*, sometimes made out of available material at the last moment. Arabs rarely fought on camel-back, these animals merely being a form of transport. Even the few horsemen often dismounted in a crisis, and infantry clearly dominated warfare. Here men would form disciplined lines, a leader sometimes using the point of an arrow to ensure the straightness of the ranks. Champions duelled between opposing armies before the main battle began, but then it was a matter of hand-to-hand combat with spears, swords and shields. The most common form of armour was the mail hauberk, though a lamellar cuirass could also be worn over the mail or on its own. Helmets were of segmented construction, like those of Byzantium or Iran, and were vulnerable to a downwards stroke. Many included mail aventails, the rings of which might be forced into the face by a blow. Aventails could also cover the face except for the eyes. The importance of shields and body armour is shown by the wounds most commonly suffered, these being to throat, face, feet and legs below the knees. The nomad Arabs did not make much use of javelins, these being *ahabish* or Yemeni weapons. The earliest Byzantine references to Arab arms emphasized their spears, swords and infantry bows. Three centuries later traditional Arab weapons such as very long cavalry spears and short-bladed infantry swords still caused comments among Iranians and Turks. Iranian-style daggers were also used by some 7th-century Arab warriors. A reference to a battle-axe may be an anachronism from earlier legends, though axes do appear in some drawings scratched on the rocks of Arabia.

Surprisingly, given the Iranians' reputation as bowmen, the Arabs were said to have learned their archery skills from Nubia. Little is, however, known about pre-Islamic Arab archery, which may have been more important in hunting than in war, though almost every male was a competent archer. In battle a few archers were often placed on the flanks as a defence against equally few cavalry who, in Arabia itself, were lightly protected and rarely used horse

*Relief carving of a Palmyrene warrior god wearing a lamellar cuirass, a short sword hung at his left hip, and leading two lions by chains. (Nat. Mus., Damascus)*

armour. One detailed account shows that when the cavalry did charge against archers almost all their horses were wounded. Another describes an archer dismounting, probably from a camel, and emptying his quiver on the ground before kneeling to take aim. Elsewhere archery was used in defence of fortifications. Most Arab bows seem to have been asymmetrical and of one-piece construction, using the same wood (*Grewia tenax*) as those of Nubia; a few expensive composite bows may have been available. Archers carried their bows behind their shoulders, as described in written sources and shown in pictorial sources, and there is no mention of bowcases. Arab archery was, in fact, a far cry from that of the devastating horse-archers of Turkish central Asia, Iran and even Byzantium.

The proportion of infantry to cavalry and the number of camels varied, but a well-equipped Meccan army of the early 7th century consisted of 3,000 camel-riding infantry of whom 700 were armoured, plus 200 cavalry and numerous baggage camels including those bearing the women's howdahs. Women, it seems, often accompanied armies to urge on their menfolk with poems, the threat of shame if they were captured by the enemy and the promise of favours in case of victory; if some pagan Arab legends are to be believed, the most attractive could even appear naked on the battlefield, offering themselves to the hero of the day! These tales might be attributed to later pious 'horror stories' were it not for the fact

that such cavorting does appear in early Arab drawings scratched on desert rocks.

On a more prosaic level, the adoption of rigid wood-framed camel saddles raised the military potential of the nomad tribes in the 2nd or 3rd centuries AD. Although warriors rarely fought on camels they could now cover greater distances and carry heavier loads or water supplies with less exhaustion to man and beast. Horses remained expensive, largely being reserved for use in war by the élite. Egypt exported these animals to Arabia from at least the 3rd century AD, and it was also around this time that selective breeding of the superb Arabian horse may have begun. Its legendary origins are sometimes traced back to King Solomon's stables, while domestication of the horse was attributed to Abraham's son Ishmael. In reality the Arabs' contribution to horse breeding was their new emphasis on quality rather than quantity, which probably reflected the fact that the climate of Arabia could not support large horse herds as seen on the central Asian steppes. Five 'strains' or blood-lines were known by the early Middle Ages, and although the pure-bred Arabian horse was smaller than that ridden by Iranian or Byzantine cavalry, it probably remains the most intelligent and courageous animal ever bred by man.

Quite when stirrups appeared in the Middle East is still debated, though they are generally believed to have arrived in the early 8th century following Arab

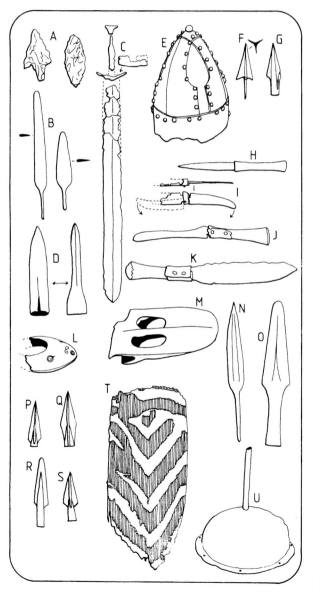

*Weaponry of the Arabian frontier: (A) stone arrowheads from Qaryat al Fau, Kinda Arab, 1–5 cents. AD (University Mus., Riyadh); (B) large knives or daggers from Oman, prob. 6–7 cents. AD (Dept. Ant., Oman); (C) sword from Oman, prob. 6–7 cents. AD (Dept. Ant., Oman); (D) spearhead from Susa, Sassanian 4 cent. AD (whereabouts unknown); (E) helmet with iron frame & bronze segments from Mosul, late Sassanian or early Arab–Islamic 7 cent. (British Mus., no. 22497, London); (F–G) bronze tang & socket arrowheads from Hatra, 2 cent. AD (Nat. Mus., Mosul); (H–K) Romano-Jewish knives from Murabba'at, early 2 cent. AD, note that the blade of knife I folds back into its handle (Archaeol. Mus., West Jerusalem); (L) bone archer's thumb-ring from Dura Europos, mid-3 cent. AD (Yale Univ. Art Gallery, Newhaven USA); (M–S) bronze axehead, tang & socket-type bronze spearheads, four socketed bronze arrowheads, from Dura Europos, mid-3 cent. AD (Yale Univ. Art Gallery, Newhaven, USA); (T) shield of canes threaded through strips of leather from Dura Europos, mid-3 cent. AD (Yale Univ. Art Gallery, Newhaven, USA); (U) bronze shield-boss from Hatra, 2 cent. AD (Nat. Mus., Mosul).*

conquests in Turkish central Asia. But less well-known evidence indicates that pre-Islamic Arabs knew of, and occasionally used, leather or wooden stirrups—although these have left no archaeological trace. Al Jahiz, writing in the 10th century, stated that some early 7th-century Arabs used stirrups,

though not of iron, and that the Prophet Muhammad told them to remove these 'Persian' signs of unmanly weakness. Instead they should vault into their saddles in the traditional Arab, and of course Roman, manner. Al Jahiz also seemed to indicate that the ancient Arabs used saddles which lacked a wooden

▼ *Mosaic showing an Arab nomad leading his camel, mid–6 cent. AD. Note the size of the bow slung across his shoulders and the long sword at his belt. This mosaic was probably* *dedicated by the Ghassanid phylarch of what is now southern Jordan (in situ Monastery church of Kayanos, Valley of Mount Nebo; Fr. M. Piccirillo photograph)*

◄ *Graffiti & Petraglyphs: (A–D) graffiti of warriors & huntsmen, Meroitic 2–4 cents. AD (in situ Great Enclosure at Musawwarat al Sufra, Sudan); (E) 'Triumph of King Silko of Nubia', graffito, Nubian 3 cent. AD (in situ Kalabsha Temple, southern Egypt; (F–G) wall painting of horseman & infantry warrior, Kinda Arab, 1–5 cents. AD, note that the faces have been erased (in situ market area, Qaryat al Fau, central Arabia); (H) 'Kahl the Wise', petraglyph, Kinda Arab, 1–5 cents. AD (in situ Tuwaiq escarpment near Qaryat al Fau, central Arabia); (I–J) battle scene with cavalrymen on armoured and* *unarmoured horses, petraglyph, pre-Islamic Oman (in situ Wadi Aday, south of Matrah); warrior with rectangular shield, petraglyph, pre-Islamic Oman (in situ Bilad Sait); (L) Arab graffito on plaster wall, 2 cent. AD (in situ Avdat, southern Israel); (M–R) petraglyphs on rocks of Syrian & Jordanian desert, pre-Islamic Arab, note long hair (M–N), two riders on one camel (O), naked woman (P), combat between horseman & camel rider (R) (after Ryckmans); (S) graffito of horseman with infantry-style quiver on his back, 3 cent. AD Romano-Palmyrene (in situ Dura Europos).*

'tree' or frame. Treeless saddles are, in fact, still made in Syria and Jordan, where they provide a perfectly comfortable seat.

The fortifications of pre-Islamic Arabia were not, of course, comparable to those of Byzantium. The mud-brick towers on stone foundations around the Kinda capital of Qaryat al Fau are sited on a defensible escarpment one kilometre from the centre of town. Within these walls were inner defences around a market area consisting of three separate walls six metres thick and with a single gate. The *utum* or fortified tribal houses in some oases relied on the height of their walls and on slings, archery and rocks piled ready on the ramparts. Some had small stone-throwing engines which could also be used against neighbouring houses, while movable 'sheds' were available to the attackers. Most stone-throwing engines were of the Graeco-Roman torsion type, Chinese-style counterweight mangonels not yet having reached the Middle East. Such devices were rarely taken on long campaigns so that the simplest wall or even a ditch lined with archers could foil a normal Arab raiding party. Such ditches were, in fact, regarded as a new-fangled and rather unfair 'Persian' idea.

# SYRIA

The Roman historian Ammianus described the peoples of Rome's frontier from Nubia to northern Mesopotamia as natural warriors and a 'dangerous nation'. Yet only recently has their importance been recognized by modern scholars, while archaeological excavation is an even more recent study. Now, however, areas like the Hawran are known to have been prosperous and quite densely populated with many villages and some fortifications.

In Syria most nomad tribes were, until modern times, sheep herders. Known as *swayeh* or semi-nomadic *ra'w*, they planted crops in autumn, grazed sheep or goats in the desert during winter, then returned to harvest their fields in spring. Such tiny fields could be deep in the seemingly inaccessible *harra*, a huge area of black basalt boulders separating the fertile lands of the west from the desert steppes or *midbar* to the east. Another remarkable feature of bedouin society during the Romano-Byzantine and early Islamic periods was widespread literacy among men and women. Here the way of life differed from that of the camel-raising *bedu* of the Arabian Penin-

*Carved ivory box from Coptic Egypt, 6–7 cents.; the figure is dressed as a nomadic Arab carrying either a short javelin or the stick used to guide a camel while riding. (British Mus., inv. 298, London)*

sula. The Syrian desert frontier was, as it is now, a marginal area where small climatic variations can significantly change the degree of vegetation. A recent theory has proposed a roughly 570-year climatic cycle. This suggests that the population was low during a hot, dry period, coinciding with the Hellenistic era, followed by a cooler, wetter period which saw higher populations in the Nabatean and early Roman centuries. Another hot, dry cycle reached its peak in the 3rd century AD, and saw significant nomad pressure against the Roman frontier as desert pasture grew poorer. Cooler and wetter centuries coincided with flourishing Byzantine and early Islamic civilizations, while a following dry period saw the decline of urban life and agriculture along the desert margins from the later 8th century.

Wherever it stood, the boundary between settled and nomadic peoples was never rigid. Rather it formed a porous zone where the two cultures co-existed in regions where life was harsh for both. The tribes to the east were transhumants rather than freely wandering nomads, and their annual migrations followed fixed routes—as they still do. People lived by hunting, fowling, gathering wild plants and milking their flocks. In winter, while they grazed their animals in desert pasture, the settled farmers grew their crops. Harvests are gathered early in the Middle East, so when the nomads migrated back into the settled zone in summer their flocks grazed the stubble and manured the farmers' fields. Meanwhile nomads and villagers exchanged products. Only when the government of an agricultural zone broke down or failure of the desert's winter grazing threatened famine were the nomads tempted to raid their richer neighbours.

Many Arab-speaking peoples also lived within the Roman and Sassanian Empires long before the Arab–Islamic expansion of the 7th century. Quite who was or was not an Arab has now been overlaid by the fierce nationalisms of the 20th century, but even in ancient times the issue was unclear. The nomads were, of course, obviously Arab—be they pagan, Christian or Jewish—but many inhabitants of the Fertile Crescent were more difficult to identify. With a few Greek or Latin exceptions, they were Semitic. Migration from the desert to the town has been a constant of Middle Eastern history, and by Roman times those who retained closest links with their

Statue of Meki Ibn Nishru, probably a nobleman of Hatra, 1–2 cents. AD. His costume is entirely Parthian in style, particularly the voluminous leggings and long padded shoes. (National Mus., Mosul)

desert ancestry were the most Arab in culture. Others had been more or less assimilated by Aramean, Hebrew or more recent Graeco-Roman civilizations.

Peoples within the Roman Middle East who could fairly be regarded as Arab were the Osroeni of Edessa (modern Urfa), the Alchaedamnus, Rhambaei, Gambarus and Themella of north-western Syria, most of the inhabitants of Palmyra, some ruling dynasties in the Orontes valley, the Ituraeans of Lebanon and what is now southern Syria, and the Jewish Idumaeans of southern Palestine of whom King

Herod is the best known. The Nabateans who excavated a staggering rock-cut city at Petra in southern Jordan were Arab, as were the tribes of Sinai and Egypt's Eastern Desert. But most of those who had adopted a settled way of life were known as 'Syrians' to the Romans, and they provided the Imperial Army with its finest archers. Some made a cultural as well as military mark. The stupendous remains of Petra and Palmyra are well known, while the rulers of Edessa made that city a centre of Semitic culture rivalling 'Greek' Antioch. The biblical role of King Herod's Idumaeans is not a happy one, but this people had an interesting history. Aramaicized, Judaized, Hellenized and ultimately Romanized, they may finally have returned to their Arab roots to re-emerge as the Judham tribe of southern Palestine. During the early Roman period many of these Arab peoples formed states which, though vassals of Rome, often warred one with another. Such petty states generally proved loyal to the Empire, but were gradually replaced by direct Roman rule. Other Arab peoples arrived during the later Romano-Byzantine period, the Ghassanids being only the last and most famous. Most were settled by the Imperial authorities as *foederati*, semi-autonomous frontier forces, as was done with Germanic tribes along Rome's northern border. As such their military forces formed part of the late Roman army (see forthcoming MAA, *Romano-Byzantine Armies 4th–9th century*).

In military terms Syria was also a frontier zone. While there was strong Central Asian influence on weaponry and tactics via the Empires of Iran, there had also been a strong Greek impact since the time of Alexander the Great. Roman influence was equally strong and is shown in a Dead Sea Scroll known as *The War of the Sons of Light and the Sons of Darkness*. Essentially it was a religious text preparing more fanatical Jewish Zealots for what they believed was the fast approaching end of the world. Its military content, though based upon Old Testament concepts, reflected Roman rather than Greek or Semitic ideas. Helmets are given Latin names, while the spear and javelin tactics are those of Roman auxiliaries rather than of a Roman legion or Macedonian phalanx. Other sources show that the Idumaean King Herod's army was very Roman in its organization.

Greek and Latin military ranks were also used by Herod's Nabatean neighbours, including the *qintryn* or 'centurion'. Romans, of course, returned the compliment by taking over Nabatean military systems intact after they occupied Arabia Petraea and faced the same conditions of desert warfare. Further north the oasis city-state of Palmyra stood midway between Graeco-Roman and Iranian-Central Asian military influences. It has been compared with Greek Sparta in its very military character and the toughness of its tiny army, but in reality Greek influence upon Palmyra was superficial—despite the soaring

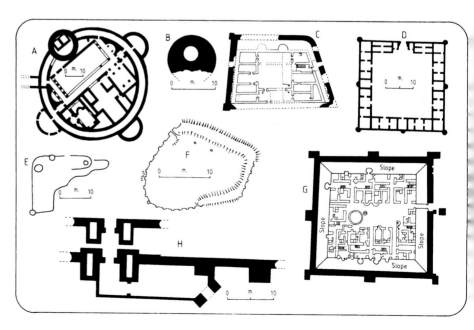

*Fortifications: (A) The Herodium, King Herod's palace near Bethlehem, 1 cent. AD; (B) Al Burg, Ghassanid Arab tower north-east of Damascus, late 6 cent. AD; (C) palace or castle in city of Hira, Lakhmid, probably 6 cent. AD; (D) Khirbat al Baydah, Ghassanid Arab 'seasonal palace' north-east of the Jebel al Arab, 6 cent. AD; (E) Al Qatr Azan, pre-Islamic Yemeni fortress, 4–6 cents. AD; (F) Al Barira, citadel in eastern Yemen, 5 cent. BC–7 cent. AD; (G) fortified market area at Qaryat al Fau, capital of the Kinda tribe, central Arabia 1–5 cents. AD; (H) northern gate of Hatra showing bent-entrance system, 2–3 cent. AD.*

North Africa, 1st–2nd Cs. BC:
1: Numidian prince, 2nd C. BC
2: Berber horseman, 1st C. BC
3: Garamante warrior, 1st C. BC

A

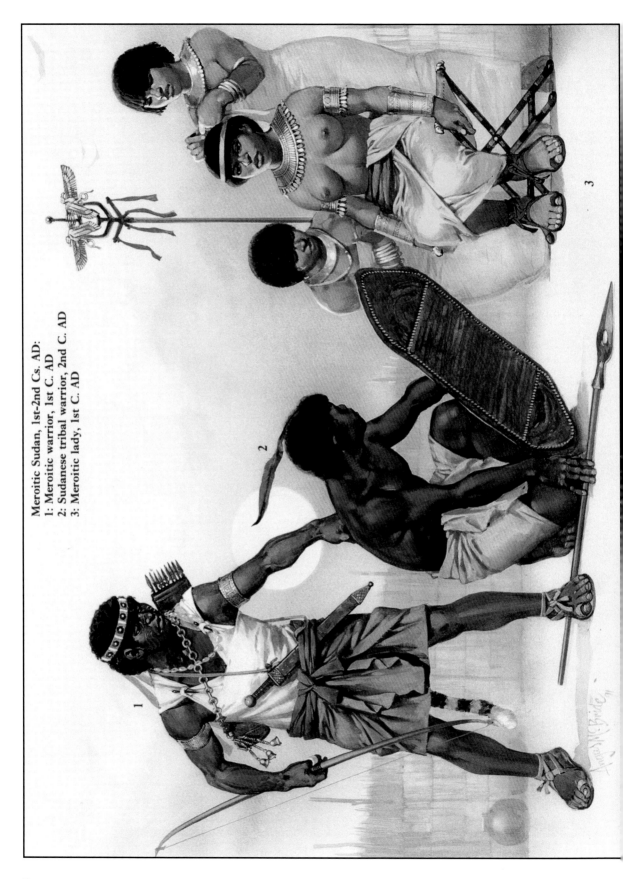

Meroitic Sudan, 1st-2nd Cs. AD:
1: Meroitic warrior, 1st C. AD
2: Sudanese tribal warrior, 2nd C. AD
3: Meroitic lady, 1st C. AD

B

Nubia, 3rd–4th Cs. AD:
1: King Silko, 3rd C. AD
2: Blemmye warrior, 4th C. AD
3: Roman frontier guard, 4th C. AD

Judaea & Arabia Petraea, 1st C. AD:
1: Nabatean camel soldier
2: Herodian horse-archer
3: Zealot 'sicarius'

D

Palmyra, 3rd C. AD:
1: Queen Zenobia
2: Palmyrene guardsman
3: King Odenathus

E

Palmyra & Hatra, 2nd-3rd Cs. AD:
1: Arab-Palmyrene soldier, 3rd C. AD
2: Hatrene clibanarius, 2nd C. AD
3: Palmyrene soldier, Dura Europos, 3rd C. AD

F

Arabia Felix & Ethiopia, 4th-6th Cs. AD:
1: Yemeni soldier, 5th C. AD
2: Ethiopian governor, 6th C. AD
3: Omani marine, 3rd-4th Cs. AD

1: Clibanarius from Ahwaz, mid-3rd C. AD
2: Tanukhid auxiliary, 4th C. AD
3: Lakhmid élite cavalryman, 6th C. AD

H

columns and temples which still stand stark against the surrounding desert. Eastern military influence was far more important. Palmyra's use of the four-horned saddle like Iranian, Roman and Nabatean cavalry is only part of the broader story of horse-harness of the Middle East. It was, however, associated with an adoption of Iranian heavy cavalry armour. Arab peoples who dominated the Syrian desert after the fall of Palmyra seem then to have adopted a Sassanian style of wood-framed saddle which could itself be linked to the history of stirrups in the Middle East.

Nabatean and Palmyrene troops helped the Romans defend the frontier and took part in Roman expeditions further afield. They also put down rebellions within Roman territory—particularly among the Jews of Palestine—while the great Jewish Revolt led to tension and banditry which permitted increased nomad infiltration. After annexing Nabatean Petra and subsequently Palmyra, Rome recruited the young men of these regions not only because of their reputation as archers but to remove a potential source of trouble. Similar motives lay behind Roman recruitment of Syrian and Jewish bandits. Meanwhile Arab tribal leaders from beyond the frontier found a role, being given houses in border villages and titles such as *strategos* or 'commander' of nomad auxiliaries. In reality such auxiliary forces were probably a myth designed to give their leaders status, for none had numbers. Meanwhile Rome played one tribe off against another, though inscriptions found deep in the desert make it clear that nomads still sometimes clashed with Roman patrols.

As far as the Romans were concerned, the tactical role of their Arab allies was to raid enemy rural areas during wars with the Parthian or Sassanian Empires, protect Roman territory from similar raids, serve as auxiliaries in the main army, police the trade routes and extend Rome's authority into Arabia, not by direct conquest but by subordinating tribes to the authority of Rome's Arab allies. A rising threat from the east, following the replacement of the Parthian Empire by that of the Sassanians, led to increasing Arab importance in Roman eyes. It was, after all, Palmyra which drove the Sassanians out of Syria in the 3rd century following Rome's defeat by these invaders. Palmyra then made its own doomed bid for domination of the area, but even after Palmyra was

*Statue of King Uthal of Hatra, 1 cent AD. In addition to leggings the king also wears a richly decorated tunic and matching Parthian cap. The hem of his long coat is draped over the scabbard of his sword. (National Mus., inv. MM8, Mosul)*

crushed Arab soldiers went on to play an increasingly important role in the Roman army and as allied auxiliaries. It was then that the new Roman frontier system evolved in which Arab tribal leaders were recognized as *phylarchs*.

## Armies of the Syrian Frontier

By the end of the 1st century BC the Nabateans had evolved from an association of clans into a stable state with a regular army and fortified posts along vital caravan routes. To their nomad tactics of sudden attack and speedy retreat the Nabatean army added defence in depth, luring invaders into desert terrain, attacking their flanks and erecting hilltop field fortification from which the enemy could be defied. The Nabatean army clearly included officer ranks, infantry and cavalry; one known force consisting of 1,000 cavalry and 5,000 infantry. Camels gave great strategic mobility, while the Nabateans were also capable of conducting proper sieges of cities like

Jerusalem. Yet it was the amazing system of communications in the southern and eastern deserts, and the Nabateans' ability to police the intractable nomads, that most impressed Rome. Arabs formed the bulk of the army but this also included Jews. Whether these came from Palestine or were descended from neighbouring peoples converted during biblical times is unknown.

Nabateans fought as allies of Rome during various Imperial campaigns, when they probably operated as horse-archers and camel-riding mounted infantry. In battle Nabatean cavalry tactics may have reflected Parthian influence, whereas the Judean armies of King Herod remained closer to Hellenistic and Roman military tradition. The Nabateans probably always had horses, while cavalry had, of course, been used in Syria for a thousand years. Yet it was their camel-mounting infantry that gave the Nabateans their military advantage. Here again a new form of saddle made the difference. To achieve maximum speed and endurance the camel rider must sit on top of the animal's hump, not behind it as seen in ancient times. The first saddle which permitted this had appeared in the 8th century BC, but the Nabateans seem to have added a rigid frame to their camel saddles. Nabatean warriors could now sling weapons, quivers, a shield, enormous saddle bags and even skins of water from the new arrangement without discomfort for the camel.

The Nabatean system of roads and outposts was almost as elaborate as that of the Romans. In addition to wells and caravanserais the Nabateans set up isolated temples along these roads, perhaps serving as financial centres for the traders who plied the routes. The deep deserts were, in reality, shared with local tribes, yet the Nabateans built forts as far east as Wadi Sirhan and as far south as Medain Salih. Here the Nabatean frontier city was surrounded by a strong wall with square towers, plus guard posts even further south. In the north and west the Nabateans re-fortified existing Iron Age watchtowers, particularly where these protected water sources. The most important northern Nabatean site was Bosra, a city founded by King Harith (Aretas) III to protect the road from Petra to Damascus. In these fertile regions the Nabateans also established agricultural settlements such as Umm al Jamal in northern Jordan.

Unlike the situation in the south, the nomadic Arab tribes of what are now southern Syria and northern Jordan kept their distance from the Nabateans and from their Jewish Herodian rivals. But after direct Roman rule was imposed they took a more active part in the defence of the Roman Empire. The Thamud tribe inherited some of the Nabateans' frontier role after making peace with Rome around AD 167. A large nomad graveyard beneath what is now Jordan's Queen Alia Airport may have been used by *foederati* of the Thamud tribe in the 2nd and early 3rd centuries. Virtually no weapons were found in this Queen Alia site, but large sheets of fine leather could have been parts of camel saddles, cloaks or even tents.

Arab tradition claims the Amalakites as Arab forerunners of a whole sequence of tribes who inherited a frontier relationship with the Roman Empire, regarding this biblical people as 'the first kingdom that the Arabs had in Syria'. Such traditions probably contain a grain of truth, as might a story that the Qudaa tribe, who took over when the Thamud declined, originally came from Yemen. They in turn were succeeded by the Tanukh, the Salih and finally the Ghassanids.

*Statue of a nobleman from Hatra, 1 cent. AD, with a long dagger on his right hip. (National Mus., inv. MM14, Mosul)*

The small armies of Rome's Middle Eastern client kings were nevertheless valuable allies for the Empire. Herod of Judea sent around 500 troops with Aelius Gallus' invasion of Arabia, the Nabateans providing a contingent of 1,000. During the First Jewish Revolt in Palestine the client states of Hims, Commagene, the Ituraeans and Nabateans provided 7,000 archers and 3,000 cavalry to fight alongside Rome's legions.

The Judaized Idumaeans, from which King Herod's dynasty sprang, were of Arab origin and their home territory lay between present-day Hebron, Beersheba and the Dead Sea. Although they had assimilated much non-Semitic civilization, they retained their military prowess. On the other hand King Herod's army was unpopular among many other peoples of Palestine. Like the Samaritans, the Idumaeans were often seen as not being 'real' Jews by descendants of the original Hebrew tribes, while King Herod's alliance with Rome was regarded as treachery by the more religious. For their part the urban Greek population of Palestine resented being ruled by a despised Jew. Only the Romans were loyal in their support of the Herodians, the Empire supplying a legion to be stationed in Palestine. Meanwhile the Herodians followed their own interests in dealings with neighbours such as the Nabateans, with whom they fought more than once. For their part the Nabateans developed close links with another client 'state' or association of cities—the Decapolis (Ten Cities) of Jordan and Syria. This Decapolis was Greek in character if only partly in population.

In AD 53 the Romans made one of the last of the Herodian dynasty, Agrippa II, Tetrarch or ruler of a non-Jewish kingdom in what is now southern Syria. After failing to dissuade his fellow Jews in Palestine from rebelling against Roman rule, Agrippa sent troops to help the Romans crush this First Jewish Revolt. By the time he died at the very end of the 1st century AD, Agrippa II had pacified the Tetrarchy of southern Syria and extended his authority eastward among the semi-nomadic tribes—whereupon the Romans annexed the Tetrarchy and incorporated its army within their own.

Quite a lot is known about the armies of these Syrian client states. Herod the Great, for example, enlisted his own Idumaean countrymen as well as

Statue of a warrior in Hatra-Parthian costume, probably from Hatra, 1–2 cents. AD. Like the other Hatrene statues this also shows a long cavalry sword worn on the left hip. (National Mus., Aleppo)

foreign settlers and nomadic tribesmen. Elite units were recruited from European Gauls (including some who had fought for Queen Cleopatra of Egypt), from Thracians and even Germans. Veterans were settled in military colonies near the frontiers which then provided a pool of trained manpower. This was the case along a narrow but rugged area of fertile valleys just east of the river Jordan which had fallen under Herod's control. Senior officers were known by Greek titles such as *archon* and *strategoi*, while Italian officers, perhaps veterans of a Roman civil war, also served Herod. A certain Volumnius held the rank of tribune, while Rufus and Gratus commanded the royal cavalry and infantry. Such men could provide the training methods needed by a Roman-style army.

The Jewish community in Parthian Iraq, descended from exiles sent to 'Babylon' in biblical times, retained close links with the Herodian dynasty and also supplied troops. One such wealthy 'Babylonian' Jew named Zamaris was appointed governor of Deraa on the present Syrian–Jordanian frontier. To police this non-Jewish area Zamaris brought 500 'Babylon' horse-archers plus their families. His grandson later trained and led the army of the Tetrarch Agrippa II, while the 'Babylonian' soldiers of Deraa continued to furnish the Herodians with cavalry. Further north and east the rugged and again non-Jewish Trachonitis area south of Damascus fell under Jewish rule for several generations, and here Herod the Great settled 3,000 loyal Idumaean troops plus 5,000 horsemen from Batanaea. Like the Nabateans, the Herodians dug water cisterns along the roads that crossed their territory and fortified vulnerable or troublesome areas. King Herod also had some immense citadels built, of which the circular Herodium near Beth-lehem and Masada on its cliff above the Dead Sea are the best known. In Jerusalem itself he rebuilt the ancient citadel dominating the Temple and erected a new fortress overlooking Jerusalem from the west.

The imposition of direct Roman rule in Judea was soon followed by the First Jewish Revolt. Many people took part, from professional soldiers to peasants, religious fanatics and bandits. The most effective were trained warriors like those who served under Josephus, a member of a priestly family from Galilee who later wrote the famous *Bellum Judaicum*, 'Jewish War'. In addition to a mercenary corps of some 2,000 non-Jewish infantry, Josephus led a Galilean Jewish peasant militia. Many of his army may also have been recruited from local bandits who had been fighting a guerrilla war against Roman occupation for years. A second leader from Galilee was John of Gischala, who was at one time said to have commanded an army of 6,000 mercenaries as well as local volunteers.

Other forces were represented by followers of the High Priest in Jerusalem and by fanatical Zealots, of

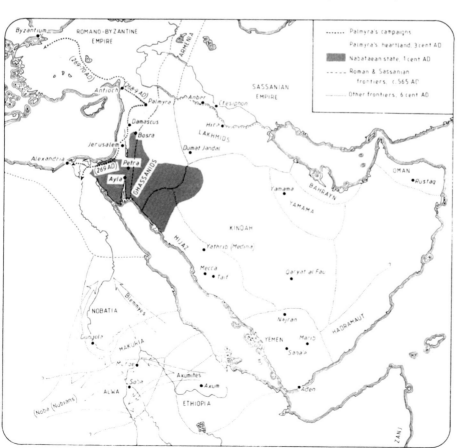

*The Middle East*
*1–6 cents. AD*

whom the *sicarii* were the most ruthless; their name is thought to stem from the Latin word *sica* meaning a curved knife. They certainly specialized in daring assassinations of Jews who collaborated with the Romans, particularly with knives or short swords hidden beneath their cloaks. But there may also be a connection between the Latinized term *sicarii* and the Semitic–Arabic word *'askar* meaning soldiers. Judas Iscariot, the disciple who betrayed Jesus, was probably a *sicarii*, while other disciples with resistance links may have been Simon the Cananaean (then a code-word for Zealot), James and John, who were called the 'sons of thunder', and even Peter, who could have been one of the Barjonim—'those outside the Law'. Some Zealots and *sicarii* escaped to Egypt after the fall of Masada and Rome's crushing of the First Jewish Revolt. There they again tried to stir up the local Jewish community, but failed and were handed over to the authorities.

The most important client state on the northern part of the desert frontier was Palmyra. Four Arab tribes dominated the area, while the names of most known Palmyrene soldiers were Arab in origin. Nomad tribes also provided Palmyra with auxiliary troops, while pagan Arab gods were included in the Palmyrene pantheon. Of these, 'Arsu, god of camels, may have been introduced from the Arabian peninsula, while 'Azizu was a horseman's god long worshipped in northern Syria. The main horse-breeding areas were, however, north-west of Palmyra where Arab influence was weakest. The indigenous costume of Palmyra was a simple tunic, but elaborate Iranian fashions, including embroidered trousers and leggings of cloth or leather, were adopted by the ruling élite. Little was owed to Greece or Rome, except perhaps some aspects of arms or armour.

All Palmyrene men went armed, élite warriors wearing long Iranian cavalry swords plus daggers on their hips, while Parthian Iran provided the model for Palmyra's army. Zenobia's husband, King Odenathus, had raised a troop of heavily armoured cavalry from his bodyguard and surrounding tribes. Palmyrene armies could be remarkably large, one supposedly consisting of 1,000 armoured cavalry and 9,000 tribal horse-archers. Basically, however, Palmyra's sources of manpower were limited, though of high quality. Following Palmyra's conquest of Roman Syria, units from Rome's III Legion were

enlisted—perhaps forcibly—into Palmyrene ranks. They played a leading role in Queen Zenobia's conquest of Roman Egypt, but later turned against Palmyra during the Roman counter-attack.

Palmyra's army was, however, originally designed for war against the Iranians, using horse-archers supported by armoured cavalry. The role of the latter was to destroy an enemy who had been disorganized, demoralized and depleted by the horse-archers. In fact the armoured troopers operated as shock cavalry, just as medieval knights would do, probably fighting in close wedge formations protected by mail and perhaps lamellar or scale armour. Most were what Romans knew as *cataphractii*, where only the rider was armoured; a minority might have been *clibanarii*, where both rider and horse wore armour. The available horses were quite strong enough to bear such loads, and there was no need of those 'cart-horse' breeds which are still wrongly thought to have carried the knights of the Middle Ages. Nor was the lack of stirrups a hindrance, as Palmyrene élite cavalrymen, like their Parthian and Roman foes, used four-horned saddles; recent research has shown these to give enough support for a rider to wield a long sword. The ultimate defeat of Queen Zenobia's armoured troopers by the lighter Roman cavalry may have been a result of superior numbers, better military organization or simply the exhaustion suffered by heavy cavalry in the heat of the desert.

In reality Palmyra's horse-archers were of greater military significance than *cataphractii* or *clibanarii*. The power of their composite bow was already likely to have been great, though there was considerable improvement of such weapons from the ancient Persian, through the Graeco-Roman to the later Turkish medieval periods. Such changes affected range and penetrating power, though perhaps not the accuracy of the bow. The tactics required of Palmyrene archers would have differed depending on whether they faced close-packed static Roman infantry, close-packed but moving groups of armoured cavalry, or dispersed, fast-moving light cavalry. One composite bow dating from the 1st century BC to 3rd century AD was found at Yrzi near the river Euphrates. It might have been typical of some weapons used along the Roman frontier, and a modern replica of this Yrzi bow suggests a draw-weight of 30–35 kgs. The forces of Palmyra also

Relief carving of Asadu and Sa'dai with an altar between, from Dura Europos, 2–3 cents. AD. Though the art of Dura Europos was cruder than that of neighbouring Palmyra the costumes, weaponry and harness shown are virtually identical. Note the apparent martingale strap running from the saddle, beneath the horse's breast strap to the bridle. (National Mus., Damascus)

employed camel-mounted troops to police the desert and patrol the trade roads, one senior officer being known as the Master of Camels. In the more fertile steppes, however, patrols may have ridden horses.

Palmyrene territory came close to the Roman frontier fortress of Dura Europos on the Euphrates. Palmyra had, in fact, strong links with Dura, and the garrison that defended this city against the Sassanians around AD 260 included Palmyrene troops. Sixteen to eighteen of the garrison were found beneath its shattered walls, along with their arms, armour and last pay, when the fortress was excavated in the 1930s. Many wore mail hauberks, and their wooden shields were painted pink with bronze bosses, one being reinforced with cross-bars. These men would, in fact, have looked much like the mailed warriors on a wall painting in a synagogue at Dura. Infantry also played a part in Palmyrene forces, garrisoning many small desert forts east of Palmyra. According to the later Roman historian Ammianus, northern Arabia was still 'filled with strong forts and castles erected by the vigilance of the former inhabitants in suitable and readily defensible ravines to repel the raids of neighbouring tribes'. Many surviving forts are, in fact, sited within wadis rather than on hilltops, probably to block such valleys, which, with their greater vegetation, could have served as migration routes for tribes with flocks.

Only after Rome crushed Palmyra with the help of neighbouring tribes did the word *saraceni* first appear; it seems to have referred specifically to the fully nomadic tribes. Among these were the Judham, rivals of Palmyra in north-eastern Jordan, and the Tanukh, who used a Nabatean form of script. All were regarded by Rome as excellent warriors and a useful source of auxiliaries and allies. A major change in Roman and Byzantine frontier defence now led to the development of the *phylarch* system, in which leaders of a dominant local tribe were recognized as military governors of the frontier zone. The most famous *phylarch* dynasties came from the Salih and Ghassanid tribes, their armies forming an integral part of late Roman and early Byzantine military structure. This system proved effective and cheap, persisting right down to the 7th century. Then a generation of Sassanian occupation and a brief Byzantine reconquest was followed by the Arab–Islamic attack which finally returned the Fertile Crescent to the authority of its own Semitic inhabitants.

# MESOPOTAMIA

On the far side of the Syrian desert, Rome's Iranian enemies also had small Arab states along their border. Hatra, for example, preserved a precarious independence under Parthian suzerainty between the rival empires in what is now north-western Iraq. During the 2nd century AD Hatra withstood two epic sieges by Roman armies. With the fall of the Parthians in Iran Hatra shifted its allegiance to Rome, but this did not save it from Sassanian conquest in the mid-3rd century.

Another Arab frontier state emerged in the later Sassanian period, this time in southern Iraq. Here the Lakhmid tribal confederation had its capital at Hira on the very edge of the desert. By this time the Sassanian Empire was developing a 'Maginot Line' siege mentality, and while the Roman Empire abandoned many of its fortified *limes* frontier zones in

*Carved relief of a warrior god in Arab–Parthian style from Dura Europos, early 3 cent. AD. Note the spear, small round shield and large sword. (Yale University Art Gallery, Newhaven, USA)*

Syria, the Sassanians erected long defensive walls in various border regions. The most famous faced Turkish attack from the north, but comparable walls and ditches were also constructed in Iraq. According to the medieval Arab historian Yaqut, this Sassanian *khandaq* or ditch included towers and fortified points with arsenals and depots to the rear. The Lakhmid capital of Hira stood near this line, while the Lakhmids' strategic role was, like that of Rome's Arab allies, to police the neighbouring desert, extend Sassanian influence into the Arabian peninsula and provide auxiliary troops.

As Sassanian power and prestige declined the

*Drawing on a section of plaster wall from Dura Europos, 3 cent. AD. The standing figure on the right appears to be dressed as a Roman with a short-sword. The horseman on the left is dressed in Parthian style with baggy trousers, a shield on his left arm and a quiver of arrows at the rear of his saddle. (Yale University Art Gallery, Newhaven, USA)*

Lakhmids grew more independent, but before they could break away entirely their dynasty was abolished by its Iranian paymasters early in the 7th century. However, the Sassanians did not fill the military gap and consequently had no desert army nor many camel-mounted troops when the Arab–Islamic tide hit them a few decades later. Some local Arabs fought in a mixed force which resisted this onslaught, but many more supported the Muslims, who were widely seen as liberators, just as they were in Syria and Egypt. Even Christian Iraqi Arabs joined the Muslims in driving the Iranians from Iraq.

### Armies of the Mesopotamian Frontier

Naturally Arab armies had a great deal in common on both sides of the Syrian desert. Like Palmyra, Hatra had a mixed population of Arabs and Aramaeans, though again the Arabs dominated in military affairs. The surrounding semi-nomadic tribes played a major role in what was known in Aramaean as the *Gunda d-'Arab*. It was nomad cavalry which broke the Roman siege of AD 137 by driving enemy horsemen back into their own camp, while Arab archers killed a man standing beside the Emperor Trajan himself. Technical forms of warfare would have been the responsibility of Arabs or Aramaeans living in the city. For example, it seems likely that petrol-based fire weapons, though more primitive than the Greek Fire of the Middle Ages, were already known in northern Iraq, where crude oil seeped naturally from the ground.

The fall of Hatra brought the Roman and Sassanian empires into direct confrontation in the Fertile Crescent. Yet this did not stop Rome's ally Palmyra from recruiting armoured cavalry inside Iran. In fact

these troops were sent by Palmyra's ally, King Worud of Ahwaz, which is perhaps the least known of the kingdoms between the Romano-Byzantine and Iranian empires. Ahwaz (now the oil-rich but war-torn Iranian province of Khuzistan) lay at the head of the Gulf between the Tigris–Euphrates delta and the mountains of Iran. It had been autonomous under the Parthians but fell beneath Sassanian rule in the mid-3rd century. King Worud's cavalry probably included *clibanarii* equipped in the Iranian manner, as described by the Roman observer Heliodurus:

'The rider is almost completely encased in bronze or iron. A one-piece masked helmet covers all his head except for eye-slits. His body from shoulders to knees is covered by a suit of small overlapping bronze or iron plates (scale or lamellar armour) which is sufficiently pliable to permit movement, and attached to his legs and feet are greaves (probably flexible leg armour rather than rigid plates). The horse is similarly covered; its head by a metal plate, its back and flanks by a blanket of thin iron plates (again scale or lamellar), its legs by knemides (felt or padded material).'

Between the fall of Hatra and the rise of the Lakhmids, other Arab tribes dominated the desert. In the second half of the 3rd century AD the Tanukh were particularly important, having supposedly fled Sassanian authority before helping Rome crush Palmyra. Their most famous leader, Imru'l Qays, was, in fact, buried within Roman territory. On the other hand the pro-Sassanian Lakhmids stemmed directly from the Tanukh. Information about other 3rd-century tribes is found in Arab legends, most such stories being rooted in reality. Many are told of King Jadhimah al Abrash, who was probably leader of the Azd tribe. He is said to have been a leper who worshipped two idols and led a powerful standing army. Other tales concern Jadhimah's mortal foe, the warrior Princess Zabba, who ruled a fortress near the present Syrian–Iraqi frontier—though she was sometimes confused with Queen Zenobia of Palmyra. One tale recalls how Jadhimah's men got inside Zabba's fortress by hiding in sacks carried by a caravan of camels. A guard on the gate prodded one sack with an ox-goad, whereupon the man inside broke wind: 'There is mischief in those sacks,' said

*Alabaster statuettes probably portraying warrior gods, from Hatra, 1 cent. AD. One figure has an apparently scale-armoured skirt, which is likely to have been an imaginary form of armour based on Roman or Greek art. Other aspects of costume and weaponry are, however, typical of Hatra. (National Mus., Mosul)*

the guard, but still let the caravan enter, whereupon Jadhimah's men seized control.

During the 4th century the Bakr and Taghglib tribes also roamed the steppes between Syria and Iraq, offering their light cavalry to whichever empire paid most. Meanwhile the Lakhmids established their rule over the deserts bordering southern Iraq. This part of the Sassanian Empire was defended by a string of frontier garrisons supported by nomad auxiliaries. Beyond the frontier lay client kingdoms of which the Lakhmids became the most important. Lakhmid leaders were also given fiefs within the essentially feudal structure of Sassanian Iraq. There may have been a wall or dyke around the central part of Lakhmid territory, though their capital at Hira had few defences of its own. Beyond Sassanian territory the Lakhmids taxed neighbouring desert tribes and raided those further afield. These nomads would, however, migrate beyond Lakhmid control if such impositions grew too heavy, or would resist by force. Another semi-legendary story relates how, at a time when Lakhmid prestige was low, the sheikh of a small tribe successfully defied al Nu'man, the flatulent king of Hira, during a tax-gathering expedition. Pricking the rump of King Nu'man's horse with his spear, he cried out: 'Go home you wind-breaking king! If I felt like shoving this spearhead up somewhere else, I could do it!'

In better times Lakhmid rulers kept hostages from subordinate tribes at Hira, while ransoms could be gained in exchange for important prisoners: one senior captive was released in exchange for 1,000 camels, two singing girls and a pile of money. The Lakhmid army itself was a formidable force, being described by Procopius as 'the most difficult and dangerous enemy of the Romans'. It was supplied by the Sassanians from their military arsenals at Ukbara and Anbar, and this may have been the source of the Lakhmids' splendid leather tents, which, unlike black woollen Arab tents, were a mark of great prestige. Lakhmid armies also copied Sassanian military organization. The king relied primarily on a force of exiles and mercenaries, of whom the *sana'i* formed a royal guard recruited from tribal outlaws now protected by the king. The *dawsar* and *shahba* garrisoned the capital, the best being known as *malha* due to the colour of their iron hauberks. The *wad'i* were probably 1,000 Iranian cavalry sent to the Lakhmids' army annually. A final group were the 500 *raha'in* hostages, young men sent by subject tribes to stay in Hira for six months, who also had to fight for the Lakhmid ruler. Close relatives of the king led military formations, commanders of divisions being called *ardaf*. Auxiliaries were supplied by subordinate tribes only when needed for a major campaign. The Lakhmids' main force again consisted of cavalry, probably armoured in Sassanian style, but infantry may have defended the capital, Hira having a simple outer wall of baked brick within which were two palaces.

### Further Reading

W. Y. Adams, *Nubia, Corridor to Africa* (London 1977)

A. R. al Ansary, *Qaryat al-Fau: A Portrait of Pre-Islamic Civilization in Saudi Arabia* (London 1982)

*Reconstruction of the Northern Gate of Hatra by the German archaeologist W. Andrae in 1911. The fortifications of this city were very strong and included a 'bent entrance' system, an advanced concept which reached Rome at a later date.*

I. Browning, *Palmyra* (London 1979)

I. Browning, *Petra* (London 1973)

D. Buxton, *The Abyssinians* (Ancient Peoples and Places series) (London 1970)

B. W. B. Fentress, *Numidia and the Roman Army: Social, Military and Economic Aspects of the Frontier Zone* (British Archaeological Reports, International Series no. 53) (Oxford 1979).

P. Freeman & D. Kennedy (eds.), *The Defence of the Roman and Byzantine East* (British Archaeological Reports, International Series no. 297) (Oxford 1986)

N. Glueck, *Deities and Dolphins: The Story of the Nabataeans* (New York 1965)

P. Hitti, *History of the Arabs* (London 1956)

A. H. M. Jones, *The Herods of Judaea* (London 1938)

M. J. Kister, *Studies in Jahiliyya and Early Islam* (London 1980)

M. Rachet, *Rome et les Berbers: Un Problème militaire d'Auguste à Dioclètien* (Bruxelles 1970)

M. Sartre, *Trois études sur l'Arabie romaine et byzantine* (Bruxelles 1982)

I. Shahid, *Rome and the Arabs: A Prolegomenon to the Study of Byzantium and the Arabs* (Washington 1984)

I. Shahid, *Byzantium and the Arabs in the Fourth Century* (Washington 1984)

I. Shahid, *Byzantium and the Arabs in the Fifth Century* (Washington 1989)

I. Shahid, *Byzantium and the Semitic Orient before the rise of Islam* (London 1988)

S. Smith, 'Events in Arabia in the 6th century AD', Bulletin of the School of Oriental and African Studies XVI (1954)

Y. Yadin, B. & C. Rabin, *The Scroll of the War of the Sons of Light against the Sons of Darkness* (Oxford 1962)

# THE PLATES

## A: North Africa, 2nd–1st centuries BC:
### A1: Numidian prince, 2nd century BC
Greek and Carthaginian influence is obvious in this man's arms and armour, though such well-equipped warriors were rare in North Africa. His helmet is probably of Carthaginian origin while his mail corslet was almost certainly imported. The shield, spear, scabbard and perhaps sword could have been manu- factured locally. (Main sources: helmet & weapons from royal grave at Al Sumaa, 2–1 cents. BC, Nat. Mus., Algiers; carved reliefs, 148–118 BC, *in situ* Chemtou, Tunisia)

### A2: Berber horseman, 1st century BC
This warrior is based upon written and pictorial evidence from North Africa rather than the dubious carvings on Trajan's Column. He wears a sheepskin over a simple tunic, is armed with javelins, and guides his horse with a single rein to a leather *bozal* or halter- bridle. (Main sources: weapons from royal grave at Al Sumaa, 2–1 cents. BC, Nat. Mus., Algiers; grave- stone from Abizar, 2 cent. BC, Nat. Mus., Algiers; statuette of Numidian rider from southern Italy, 3–2 cents, BC, Louvre Mus., Paris)

### A3: Garamante Saharan desert warrior, 1st century BC
This figure is almost entirely based upon a compa- rison of written sources with later traditional cos- tume. He has the *litham* face-covering worn by many Saharan tribesmen and the skin cloak associated with the most isolated tribes. His spear, with distinctive holes in the blade, was made in the Sudan, and he is otherwise armed with a sling. The huge leather shield would later be known as a *lamt*.

## B: Meroitic Sudan, 1st–2nd centuries AD:
### B1: Meroitic warrior, 1st century AD
This warrior's longbow is similar to some seen in ancient Egypt, while his costume also seems to be within ancient Egyptian tradition. His sword reflects Greek or Roman influence, but the rest of his equipment, including the animal's tail hanging down his back, is distinctly Sudanese. (Main sources: graffiti, 1 cent. BC–3 cent. AD, *in situ* Musawwarat al Sufra Temple, Sudan; archery equipment from Meroitic graves, Nat. Mus., Khartoum; relief carving of Prince Arikankharer, 1 cent. AD, Art Mus., Worcester, Mass.; rock relief of King Sherkharer, *in situ* Jebel Qeili; Meroitic relief carvings, *in situ* Lion Temple, Naqa).

### B2: Sudanese tribal warrior, 2nd century AD
Simply armed warriors appear in much Meroitic art. They are characterized by a broad-bladed spear, a large oval shield, a long feather thrust into their hair,

and they represent the tribal warriors who formed the bulk of Meroitic and neighbouring Sudanese armies. Comparable shields were used in southern Sudan into the 20th century. (Main sources: spearhead from Meroe, Nat. Mus., Khartoum; graffiti, 1–4 cents. AD, *in situ* Musawwarat al Sufra Temple, Sudan; statuettes of bound prisoners, Meroitic 1 cent. AD, Nat. Mus., Khartoum & British Mus., London)

### B3: Meroitic lady, 1st century AD

In some respects Meroe was a matriarchal society. The costume of this aristocratic lady again has something in common with ancient Egypt, as does her jewellery. The standard is a hypothetical reconstruction based upon an object found at Meroe to which golden vultures, like those seen in Meroitic art, have been added. (Main sources: carved reliefs, *in situ* Lion Temples at Naqa & Musawwarat al Sufra; iron object from Meroe, Nat. Mus., Khartoum)

### C: Nubia, 3rd–4th centuries AD:
### C1: King Silko of Nubia, 3rd century AD

The only illustration of King Silko shows him triumphing over his foes and is clearly based upon Roman art. Yet Nubian ceremonial also imitated that of Rome, so the king may have worn any Roman regalia he could find, and this would include the mail shirt shown here. The king has otherwise been given a crown, weapons, shield, shoes and magnificent horse harness found in the royal graves at Ballana. His short sword is a distinctive weapon, while the decorated leather shield is almost identical

to those used by Beja warriors in the 19th century. (Main sources: graffito of King Silko, *in situ* Temple of Kalabsha south of Aswan; royal regalia, weaponry and horse harness from Ballana Tombs, Archaeol. Mus., Cairo)

### C2: Blemmye warrior, 4th century AD

This humble warrior is also equipped with weaponry found at Ballana. The silver bracer on his left wrist is of royal quality, as is his elaborate quiver, but the

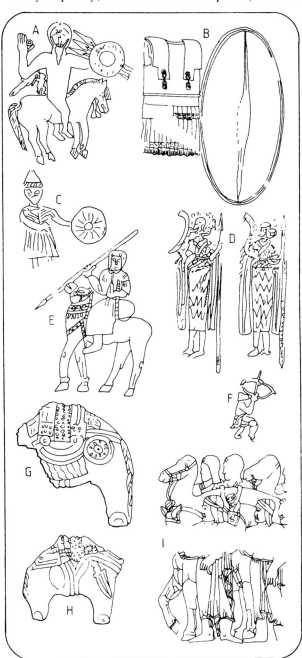

*Carvings & ceramics: (A) Berber Numidian gravestone from Abizar, 2 cent. BC (Nat. Museum, Algiers); (B) 'Triumph' carved relief of trophies, Numidian 148–118 BC (in situ Chemtou, Tunisia); (C) Libyan relief carving from Tripolitania, late 3 cent. AD (Archaeol. Mus., No. 310, Istanbul); (D) carved relief of figures with crossed straps on chest, spears, straight & curved daggers at waist, pre-Islamic southern Yemen (in situ temple of Attar, near al Hazm: after J. Ryckmans & R. B. Serjeant); (E) gravestone of Ajlam ibn Sa'dilat, dedicated to goddess Ishtar, pre-Islamic Yemen 5–6 cents. AD (location unknown: after Jawad Ali); (F) carved relief of huntsman, 2–3 cents. AD, southern Yemen (in situ Husn al Urr, Hadramaut); (G–H) fragments of ceramic camel riders, Nabatean 1 cent. BC– 2 cent. AD, note shield & sword hung from saddles (after P. J. Parr); 'Arab tribesmen bringing tribute to Sassanian Emperor Bahram II', carved rock-relief AD 277–293, note that the middle of this panel has been worn away by water erosion (in situ Bishapur, Iran).*

*Wall painting of a horse-archer from Dura Europos, 2–3 cents. AD. (National Mus., Damascus)*

The man's hair, pulled into long ringlets, would be typical of Arab peoples for many centuries, as would his simple costume of two large pieces of cloth. (Main sources: carving of warrior, 2 cent. AD, *in situ* Temenos Gate, Petra; fragments of ceramic camel riders from Petra, 1–2 cents. AD, private coll.; Syrian ivory scabbard & hilt, 2 cent. AD, Nat. Mus., Damascus)

### D2: Herodian (Idumaean) horse-archer, 1st century AD

No contemporary illustrations of Jewish soldiers seem to exist, despite thousands of imaginary reconstructions which have featured in Christian art over the past two thousand years. This man is based on written information and surviving pieces of military equipment from Palestine and surrounding regions. Here the dominant military fashions were late Hellenistic and Parthian–Iranian. The man is armed with a long sword and a powerful composite bow, both his bowcase and quiver being fastened to his saddle. His bronze helmet is shaped like a Phrygian cap, and his body is protected by a cuirass of silvered scales over which are painted iron shoulder pieces and a decorative beaten gold 'breastplate'. This latter item might, however, have been a religious rather than military costume. On his legs are laminated bronze protections including bronze slippers. The motif on the man's shield is taken from a Roman Triumph scene celebrating the capture of Jerusalem. (Main sources: west Parthian helmet, Mus. of Fine Arts, Boston; fragments of silvered cuirass & gold 'breastplate' from Masada, Israel Archaeol. Mus., West Jerusalem; carved reliefs, 1 cent. AD, *in situ* Arch of Titus, Rome)

### D3: Zealot 'Sicarius', 1st century AD

In complete contrast to the Herodian soldier, this assassin wears the Greek-influenced peasant costume of early Roman Palestine. His only weapon is a knife with a folding blade, remarkably similar to the later Spanish *navaja*. (Main sources: cloak, tunic, sandels & knife from Massada, 1 cent. AD, Israel Archaeol. Mus., West Jerusalem)

### E: Palmyra, 3rd century AD:
### E1: Queen Zenobia of Palmyra

In stark contrast to Jews or Nabataeans, the people of

stone thumb-ring was a common object. The way he has thrust poisoned arrows into his head-band was described by various observers and appears on the Emperor Constantine's Triumphal Arch—Blemmye warriors having fought for the emperor. (Main sources: weaponry from Ballana Tombs, Archaeol. Mus., Cairo; relief carving of 'African archers' on Arch of Constantine, early 4 cent., *in situ* Rome)

### C3: Roman frontier guard from Dodekaschoenos, 4th century AD

Some Roman auxiliaries may have remained in northern Nubia when Rome ceded it to the Nubians. This man is a typical late Roman cavalry soldier, though based on specifically Romano-Egyptian sources. (Main sources: helmet from Egypt, 4–5 cents. AD, Coptic Mus., Cairo; 19 cent. reproduction of lost early 4 cent. Roman 'Triumph' wall paintings in Luxor Temple, Griffith Instit., Oxford)

### D: Judaea and Arabia Petraea, 1st century AD:
### D1: Nabataean camel soldier, 1st century AD

The Nabataeans, like the Jews and Muslims, rarely portrayed the human figure; this warrior is therefore based on written descriptions and a few fragmentary illustrations. He is armed with a simple bow made of bamboo but also has a Graeco-Roman type of sword, a leather shield, and a quiver of javelins hanging from his saddle. This new form of Nabataean saddle has a wooden frame and is perched on top of the hump.

Palmyra produced wonderfully detailed statues and relief carvings of their ruling élite and ordinary people. The only known picture of Queen Zenobia shows her in Graeco-Roman style on a tiny coin. Here, however, she has been given the jewellery and costume of a high-ranking Palmyrene lady as shown in the finest Palmyrene art. Similarities between the basic costume and that of the Arab–Islamic medieval Middle East is striking. (Main sources: statues from Palmyra, 2–3 cents. AD, Palmyra Mus. & Nat. Mus., Damascus)

### E2: Palmyrene guardsman, early 3rd century AD

Some scholars have described the armour given to Palmyrene war-gods as 'Roman' and thus unreliable; but most of it seems more Hellenistic than Roman, and may well reflect the styles seen in some Middle Eastern client states. This guardsman has a tall helmet which has been attributed to Syrian auxiliaries in Roman service. His cuirass is of lamellar armour, which was rarely used by Roman troops, while the embroidered *pteruges* dangling from his shoulders and waist are equally Hellenistic. The rest of his attire is very Parthian in appearance. (Main sources: auxiliary helmet, 2 cent. AD, Archaeol. Mus., Zagreb; statues & relief carvings from Palmyra, 2–3 cents. AD, Palmyra Mus. & National Mus., Damascus)

### E3: King Odenathus of Palmyra

Here the king's costume is based upon the male counterparts of the ladies who form the basis of our reconstruction of Queen Zenobia. The influence of Parthian–Iranian fashion is, however, far stronger. Of particular interest are the king's long sword suspended from a belt secured by a button, and the metal 'suspenders' which fasten the over-leggings to the hem of his tunic. (Main sources: statues & relief carvings from Palmyra, 2–3 cents. AD, Palmyra Mus. & National Mus., Damascus)

### F: Palmyra and Hatra, 2nd–3rd centuries AD:
### F1: Arab–Palmyrene soldier, 3rd century AD

The costume and equipment of ordinary Palmyrene soldiers was naturally less sumptuous than that seen at court. This man has much in common with his Nabataean predecessor though his basic costume is less obviously Arabian. Note the archer's finger guard secured to his right hand. The fact that his quiver is on his back suggests that most shooting was on foot. Other weapons, such as a shield and sword, are again slung from his richly decorated saddle. (Main sources: statues & relief carvings from Palmyra, 2–3 cents. AD, Palmyra Mus. & National Mus., Damascus)

### F2: Hatrene clibanarius, 2nd century AD

Parthian influence was stronger in Hatra than Pal-

*Facsimile of a wall-painting showing the Philistines' capture of the Ark from the Israelites in a 3 cent. AD synagogue at Dura Europos. The horsemen of both armies are unarmoured and carry only spears, while the infantry on both sides wear mail hauberks with long and short sleeves, some also having complete mail coifs on their heads, but no other helmets are shown. All the swords are short. The shields are elongated, six-sided, with lines across probably indicating some form of strengthening. Some have small bosses. (Yale University Art Gallery, Newhaven, USA. The original of this wall painting is in the Syrian National Mus., Damascus)*

myra. This man is based upon statues of Hatrene nobles and rulers, plus Parthian or very early Sassanian armour found at Dura Europos. Beneath his quilted Parthian cap with its heraldic crescent motif he has a two-piece helmet with a mail aventail. Beneath his quilted tunic there is also a mail hauberk, while at his side he carried a relatively short sword. On the other hand his long bamboo-hafted spear seems more Arab than Parthian. Note that his bowcase and quiver are still attached to the horned saddle rather than being slung from a waist belt as done by medieval horse-archers. (Main sources: statue of King Uthal of Hatra & other statues or statuettes, from Hatra, 1–2 cents. AD, Nat. Mus., Mosul, & Nat. Mus., Aleppo)

## F3: Palmyrene soldier of Dura Europos garrison, 3rd century AD

The full mail hauberk with integral coif worn by this soldier is strikingly similar to those of early medieval European warriors, indicating the great degree of late Roman influence upon the troops of the Middle East and western Europe. His short stabbing sword is very Roman, but his large shield of reeds bound with strips of leather was specifically Mesopotamian and would be seen in Baghdad several centuries later. (Main sources: armour, weapons and shield from Dura Europos, 3 cent. AD, Yale University Art Gallery, Newhaven; 'Battle between Israelites & Philistines' on synagogue wall-painting from Dura Europos, 3 cent. AD, Nat. Mus., Damascus)

## G: Arabia-Felix and Ethiopia, 4th–6th centuries AD:

### G1: Yemeni-Arab soldier, 5th century AD

The art of pre-Islamic Yemen shows an interesting mixture of Arab and Romano-Byzantine costume and weaponry. This man has been given an imported form of unusual early Byzantine helmet which may also have been the prototype of the medieval salet. His shield is taken from a Yemeni carving but also betrays Roman military influence. His dagger and sword are, however, characteristic of his own region. The sword has the bronze grip seen in both pre-Islamic and early medieval Arab weapons, while the flag is based upon a written description of a banner carried by tribesmen from Hadramawt two centuries later. (Main sources: relief carving from Zafar, 3 cent.

AD, Archaeol. Mus., Sana'a; bronze sword-grip from Qaryat at Fau, 1–5 cents. AD, University Mus., Riyadh; relief carvings on Arch of Constantine, early 4 cent. in situ Rome)

## G2: Abraha, Ethiopian governor of Yemen, 6th century AD

A Byzantine ambassador described the gilded weaponry and jewellery of an Ethiopia ruler or governor in great detail. To this has been added information from Yemeni carvings showing the elaborate chest straps, and an early Islamic painting of the Negus of Ethiopia which again emphasizes the golden collar associated with Ethiopian kings. (Main sources: relief carving on Temple of 'Attar, in situ Jawf ibn Nasir, Yemen; wall painting of 'Negus', early 8 cent. AD, in situ Qusayr 'Amra, Jordan)

## G3: Bayasirah marine from Oman, 3rd–4th centuries AD

The only illustrations of pre-Islamic warriors in Oman are very crude rock drawings. To this may be added earlier illustrations of Omanis in Iranian art. Links between Oman and northern India were also very close, so this man has been given a scale helmet recently found in Pakistan and the quilted jerkin and dagger as shown in northern Indian art of the period. His long Sassanian-type sword was, however, found in Oman. (Main sources: helmet from Shaikhan-Dheri, probably in Lahore Mus., Pakistan; sword from Oman, 3–7 cents. AD, Dept. of Antiquities, Oman)

## H: Iran's desert neighbours, 3rd–6th centuries AD:

### H1: Clibanarius from Ahwaz, mid-3rd century AD

The people of Ahwaz were, and remain, partly Arab and partly Iranian. The military equipment in the pre-Islamic period does, however, seem to have been fully within the Iranian tradition. This man has a two-piece iron helmet with a mail aventail. His full mail hauberk has a Sassanian heraldic emblem made of bronze rings on the chest, while his sword is typical of the early Sassanian period. The voluminous leggings which cover his feet must have made walking difficult. Meanwhile he still uses the four-horned saddle. The horse-armour is of lamellar rather than scale (as found at Dura Europos), which may have been a Parthian characteristic. The horse's quilted leggings are hypothetical as no illustrations of these objects, known in Greek as *knemides*, are known. (Main sources: rock-relief of Parthian rider on armoured horse, 1–3 cents. AD, *in situ* Tang-i Sarvak, Iran; early Sassanian helmet & armour from Dura Europos, 3 cent. AD, Yale Univ. Art Gall., Newhaven; 'Triumph of Bahram II', rock relief late 3 cent. AD, *in situ* Bishapur)

### H2: Tanukhid tribal auxiliary, 4th century AD

A number of unique early Sassanian rock reliefs show Arabs bringing tribute to the Iranian emperor. Their most interesting feature is the head-cloth or *kefiyah*, a head-covering now universally associated with Arab peoples but otherwise virtually unknown in pre-Islamic and medieval Arab art. This man has also been given a narrow-bladed spear found in a late-Sassanian site in southern Mesopotamia, while his sword must also have been obtained from a Sassanian arsenal. (Main sources: spearhead from Susa, 3–5 cents., present whereabouts unknown; 'Triumph of Bahram II', rock relief late 3 cent. AD, *in situ* Bishapur)

### H3: Lakhmid Sana'i élite cavalryman, 6th century AD

Written sources state that the best units of the Lakhmid army were normally equipped from Sassanian arsenals. Consequently this man wears the Arab–Iraqi costume shown in the Bishapur rock-reliefs, but is armed with a late Sassanian (or possibly very early Islamic) helmet from Iraq and a mail hauberk found on the body of a Sassanian or allied soldier at Dura Europos. Extraordinarily long swords were also attributed to the Sassanians and their allies, but until the actual weapon thrust behind this man's saddle was recently discovered at Aphrodias in Turkey their size was assumed to have been exagge-

Some of the carvings of pagan warrior gods from Dura Europos are more Graeco-Roman in appearance, as shown here. (Yale University Art Gallery, Newhaven, USA)

rated. Note also the primitive stirrups. Some written sources suggest that these were known in the Arab world by the late 6th century, while just such wood-and-leather stirrups were used in Russia and the Caucasus until modern times. (Main sources: 'Triumph of Bahram II', rock relief late 3 cent. AD, *in situ* Bishapur; helmet from Mosul area, late 6–early 7 cents. AD, British Museum; sword from Aphrodias, present whereabouts unknown)

# INDEX

(References to illustrations are shown in **bold**. Plates are shown with caption locators in brackets.)

Agrippa II 35
Ahwaz 40, **H1** (46–47)
Alwa 12
Amalakites, the 34
Arabs 3, 10, **11**, 17, 17–18, **21**, **43**
  appearance **12**, 17, 18, **22**
  archery 19
  fortifications 22
  horses 20
  in Mesopotamia 39, 40–41
  organisation 18–19, 20
  in Syria 23–24, 33
armour 15, **17**, 18, **19**, 19, 38, **40**, **A1** (42), **43**,
  **D2** (44), **45**, **E2** (45), **F2–3** (45–46), **H1** (46),
Axum 13, 14

'Babylonian' Jews 36
Bakr, the 41
Bedouin, the 3, 16, 22
Berbers, the 3, 6, **7** (map), 7, 9
  cavalry **4**, 7, 8, 9, **A2** (42), **43**
  organisation 6–7, 8
  tactics 7–9
Blemmye, the **7**, 10, 11–12, **C2** (43–44)
Byzantium 3, 14, 15

camels 4, 9, 10, **15**, 18, 19, 20, **21**, 33, 34, 38, **D1** (44)
*cataphractii* 37
Christianity 4, 11, 16
chronology 4–7
*clibanarii* 37, 40, **F2** (45–46), **H1** (46–47)
climatic variations 23
cultural influences 4, 11, 14, 24, 33, 42, 45, 46

Dodekaschoenos 9–10, **C3** (44)
Dura Europos **38**, 38, **39**, 44, 45, 47

Egypt, raids on 11, 12
elephants 4, 11, 13
Ethiopians, the **11**, 11, 13–14
  in Arabia 14, 15, 16, **G2** (46)

fortifications 3–4, **10**, 11, 16, 22, **24**, 34, 36, 38,
  38–39, 41

Garamantes, the 9, **A3** (42)
Gauls 35
Germans 35
Ghassanids, the **24**, 24, 38
graffiti **21**

Hatra and the Hatrenes **23**, **24**, 33, **34**, **35**, 38, 39, **40**,
  41, **F2** (45–46)

helmets **8**, 19, **20**, 24, **A1** (42), **D2** (44), **E2** (45),
  **F2** (45–46), **H1** (46)
Herodian forces **24**, 35–36, **D2** (44)
Hijaz 16, 18
Hira 41
horses **15**, 15, 20, 34, **H1** (46–47)
hostages 41

Idumaen, the **23**, **24**, 24, 35–36, **D2** (44)
Iraq 38, 39, 41
Islam, emergence of 17

Jadhimah al Abrash 40–41
Jewish Arab tribes 16, 18
Jewish Revolt, the 33, 35, 36–37
Josephus 36

Kinda, the **12**, 17, **21**, 22, **24**

Lakhmids, the **24**, 38–39, 40, 41, **H3** (47)
literacy 22

Meroe and Meroitic forces **5**, **6**, 10, 11, **21**,
  **B** (42–43)
Middle East, the **36** (map)

Nabataeans, the **15**, 24, 33, 33–34, 35, **36** (map),
  **43**, **D1** (44)
Najran, Yemen 15
Noba, the 10, 11, 12, **21**, **A1** (42), **43**
nomads 16, **21**, **22**, 22, 23, 33, 34, 37, 39, 41
Nubia and the Nubians 4, 10. *see also* Noba, the
Numidia and the Numidians 3, 7, **8**

officers 35–36
Oman and Omani forces **10**, 14, 15, 16, **G3** (46)
organisation
  Arabic 18–19, 20
  Berber 6–7, 8
  Ethiopian 13
  Idumaen 24
  Lakhmid 41
  Meroitic 11
  Nabatean 33
  Palmyrene 37

Palmyra and Palmyrene forces 3, **15**, **17**, **18**, 24,
  33, **36** (map), 37–38, 39–40, **E** (44–45), **F1** (45),
  **F3** (46)
Petra 13, 14, 24, 33
*phylarch* system, the 38
prisoners **6**

Red Sea, the 11–12, 14
religion 4, 11, 13, 16, 16–17, 37
Roman Empire, the 9–10, 24, 35, 38
  frontiers 3–4, 23, 24, 33, **36** (map), 38–39
Roman forces 14, **C3** (44)
  service in 4, **7**, 24, 33, 34, 35, 44

saddles 21–22, 33, 37
Sahara, the 7, 9, 10
Salih, the 38
*saraceni*, the 38
Sassanian Empire, the 4, 11, 14–15, 16, 17, 33,
  **36** (map), 38–39, 41, 47
shields 9, **17**, 19, 38, **39**, **43**, **A1** (42), **A3** (42),
  **B2** (42–43), **D2** (44), **45**, **F3** (46)
*sicarii* Zealots 37, **D3** (44)
sieges 33–34
Silko, Nubian King 12, **21**, **C1** (43)
stirrups 20–21, **H3** (47)
Sudan and the Sudanese 3, 4, 10, 12–13, **B2** (42–43)
Syria 4, 22–24

tactics
  Arab 17–18
  Berber 7–9
  Nabatean 33, 34
  Palmyrene 37
  Yemeni 15
Taghglib, the 41
Taif 16
Tanukh and Tanukhid forces 40, **H2** (47)
Thamud, the 34
Thracians 35
trade 3, 16
'Troglodytes' 12–13

weapons **8**, 9, 11, 12, 13, 15, **17**, 18, 19, **20**, 24, **43**,
  **D2** (44)
  bows **5**, 12, 19, 37, **B1** (42), **44**
  fire 39
  javelins 9, **14**
  stone throwing engines 22
  swords **8**, 9, 14, **35**, **39**, **45**, **G1** (46), **G3** (46),
  **H3** (47)
women 20, **21**, **B3** (43), **E1** (44–45)

'X Group' culture 12

Yemen and Yemeni forces **10**, 13, 14, 15, 16, **24**, **43**,
  **G1–2** (46)

Zealots 36–37, **D3** (44)
Zenobia, Queen of Palmyra 3, 11, **16**, 37, **E1** (44–45)